100 BACKYARD ACTIVITIES

THAT ARE THE DIRTIEST, COOLEST, CREEPY-CRAWLIEST EVER!

BECOME AN EXPERT ON BUGS, BEETLES, WORMS, FROGS, SNAKES, BIRDS, PLANTS AND MORE

COLLEEN KESSLER

AWARD-WINNING EDUCATOR AND FOUNDER OF RAISING LIFELONG LEARNERS

PAGE STREET
PUBLISHING CO.

PAGE STREET
PUBLISHING CO.

First published in 2017 by

Page Street Publishing Co.

27 Congress Street, Suite 105

Salem, MA 01970

www.pagestreetpublishing.com

Distributed by Macmillan, sales in Canada by The Canadian Manda Group.

20   19   18   17   1   2   3   4

ISBN-13: 978-1-62414-373-1

ISBN-10: 1-62414-373-3

Library of Congress Control Number: 2016915842

Cover and book design by Page Street Publishing Co.

Photography by Melissa Lennig, page 32 by Shutterstock

Printed and bound in China

Page Street is proud to be a member of 1% for the Planet. Members donate one percent of their sales to one or more of the over 1,500 environmental and sustainability charities across the globe who participate in this program.

FOR TREVOR, MOLLY, LOGAN AND ISAAC

MY FAVORITE BACKYARD BIOLOGISTS.

FOR BRIAN

MY ROCK.

AND FOR SMART KIDS EVERYWHERE

STAY CURIOUS ALWAYS.

INTRODUCTION
GETTING OUTSIDE!

ARE YOU READING THIS BOOK RIGHT NOW INSIDE YOUR HOME? Yes? Well, go outside, find a nice shady spot where you can hear the birds chirping and read it there. Really! Right now. I'll wait. Unless you're in a book store . . . then buy this book first, and then take it outside with you!

Listen. You spend so much time inside these days—going to school, doing things around the house, watching TV, connecting with friends on a shared server to play a game, surfing the web on phones and tablets.

When you put away the video games, close down the computer and turn off the television to head outside, you actually can make yourself smarter. I'm serious. Studies show that being outside around nature can make you calmer, more peaceful, more attentive and even increase creativity and inventiveness.

I don't know about you, but I want to be creative, and being inventive sounds pretty cool, too.

Good scientists are both of those things.

They're creative. They're inventive. They're also curious explorers who never completely have to grow up. Imagine that—doing a job that's actually like play. Pretty awesome!

Scientists are not—no matter what you've heard—funny guys with crazy hair, hiding out in a lab somewhere. Nope! They are real, everyday people just like you and me.

SCIENCE IS PLAY.

It's questioning. It's wondering. It's exploring. And, it's testing things out to see what happens and learning from those results.

Science is really, really cool. And it's all around us.

Scientists scale mountains, dig in the dirt, create, discover and grow. They are just like you. In fact, most scientists probably started out learning about science as a kid like you. Someone who would pick up a book full of experiments that they could do in their yard with their friends, brothers and sisters, babysitters, grandmas, grandpas, parents or all alone to pass the time.

Listen . . . smart people are not the ones with all the answers. They're the ones with all the questions. And they're the ones who are out there looking for the answers to those questions.

BE SMART.
BE CURIOUS.
BE ADVENTUROUS.

And, take this book outside and experiment with all of the nature you have around you.

There is no telling what you'll discover.

So, grab a few supplies, an investigative mind and some friends, then head outside—whatever the weather—and explore. Most of the activities, experiments, crafts and projects in this book can be done with things you can find around the house. There may be a few things you need to plan ahead for, or ask an adult to help you with. This is one of those times it is a great thing to be a kid that reads ahead!

Make sure you read the directions carefully and keep yourself safe. While you're keeping yourself safe, pay attention to the way you're interacting with nature, too. Treat plants and animals with respect, and return everything to the way you found it.

Nature is amazing. And it should be respected—even as you explore to see how it works.

You can do it. You can be a great backyard biologist!

The world is waiting for your discoveries.

~ Colleen

HOW TO USE THIS BOOK
TIPS FOR BEING THE BEST BACKYARD SCIENTIST EVER!

So, you got this book. Hooray! I'm so excited for you! We're going to have a blast, and learn lots of cool things about our world together. There are a few things we need to chat about first, though, about the different things you'll be doing once you head out into the yard.

You probably noticed that the Backyard Entomology chapter is a bit bigger than the other chapters in the book. There's a reason for that. Creepy-crawly insects, arachnids and annelids (worms) are really easy to find no matter where you live in this world. They're easy and safe to handle, too. Because of that, there are a lot more activities you can do in your yard with those creatures than any other ones I could tell you about.

But, I know that there is going to come a time when you open the book to try an activity, and you're going to be annoyed with me. "But, Colleen, I can't find a bess beetle in my yard! I can only find a strawberry sap beetle . . . or a Japanese beetle . . . or a ground beetle!"

Imagine I'm right there with you. Here's what I'd say: "It's okay. Use that one instead! You're a scientist. See how that particular beetle does in the activity. You'll still learn a lot from whatever animals are around you."

So, here's the thing . . . whatever you do, stay outside. Explore. Discover. Experiment. Create. There are insects, worms, reptiles, plants and amphibians everywhere. Be creative and innovate. Use whatever you can find.

I live in the Midwest part of the United States. This past spring, while I was working on the photos for this book, it was really hard to find frogs because the weather was really strange. Usually I can find and catch green frogs all the time. Not this year. I could only find teeny-tiny tree frogs (who didn't want to cooperate for the races) and two American toads.

Seriously. We looked for weeks and only found TWO toads.

In the meantime, friends of mine from different parts of the country were complaining about all the lizards they kept trapping in their family room. A different climate can make a big difference, but I know you can find something to explore.

The most important thing you can do for yourself is to let this book be your trail guide as you explore your world. Don't have a big backyard? That's okay! Ours is small, and we can do most of these activities in it. Don't have a backyard at all? That's okay, too. You can find birds in the city, bugs on the sidewalk and plants in the corner lot. Nature is everywhere—even if we don't always pay attention.

We love exploring new places, too. Maybe you can use this book to inspire your family to go on walks around your neighborhood together. Put some bug boxes in your pocket, and bring back some little critters. Is there a nature center or a state park nearby? Try exploring there and bringing this book along.

The possibilities are endless, my friend, and you're going to be so tuned-in to nature that you're never going to want to head back inside.

So, let's go build your brain. Remember—getting outside makes you smarter! You'll be a super smart power thinker and explorer by the end of this book.

LET'S GO EXPLORE AND DISCOVER TOGETHER!

BACKYARD BIOLOGY

(BĪ-'Ä-LE-JĒ)

THINGS THAT CREEP, CRAWL, FLY AND GROW

All those things that you see moving around in your yard—bugs, birds, slugs and squirrels—they're all things biologists study. They explore plants, too. Biology is the study of all the living things you can find in the world, and it's divided into specialized fields. That means that each biologist focuses their life's work on one specific type of living thing.

AMAZING!

What would you study if you could devote your whole life to learning everything about it?

I once met a scientist whose entire life's work was understanding the eastern tent caterpillar. A caterpillar! Isn't that fantastic? He didn't even worry all that much about them in their adult form of the lappet moth—he was concerned mostly with their habits as caterpillars.

Such a super interesting thing to get to explore endlessly.

Have you gone exploring lately? What have you observed? When you look closely at the things around you, make observations and wonder about the things you see, you're thinking like a scientist.

YOU'RE A BACKYARD BIOLOGIST!

Every great scientist and naturalist needs some tools to help them as they explore and discover their surroundings. They use special words to help them classify the plants and animals they find—and wherever possible, I've included those scientific names for you to learn. Won't your friends be impressed if you tell them you spent the summer *Lepidoptera* catching? (You'll have to read on to find out what that means!)

In this section, you'll get ready to head outside by making a tool kit for discovering and recording your finds. Let's get started!

11

AMAZING NATURE EXPLORER'S JOURNAL

THE NOTEBOOKS OF GREAT SCIENTISTS THROUGHOUT HISTORY HAVE BEEN BUILT UPON IN EVERY GENERATION. WHAT YOU RECORD TODAY MIGHT BE THE OBSERVATION THAT SPARKS A NEW UNDERSTANDING TEN YEARS FROM NOW. SERIOUSLY! YOU NEVER KNOW WHAT WILL COME OF JOTTING DOWN THE STRANGE THING YOU SAW A BEETLE DOING IN YOUR YARD . . . OR HOW BIG THAT ANTHILL WAS . . . OR HOW THE CHICKADEE'S FEET FELT AS IT PERCHED ON YOUR HAND AND ATE SEED FROM YOUR PALM.

SO, START BY MAKING THE BEST NATURE JOURNAL EVER—ALL FROM THINGS AROUND THE HOUSE—AND RECORD THE THINGS YOU DO AS YOU READ THIS BOOK AND EXPLORE YOUR BACKYARD. YOUR OBSERVATIONS ARE AS UNIQUE AS YOU ARE—AND SO THEY NEED AN AMAZING JOURNAL TO BE WRITTEN INTO!

MATERIALS

Cereal box

Scissors

Paper for the inside pages

Decorative paper

Ruler

Pen

Glue stick, tape runner or double-sided tape

Heavy needle and embroidery floss, twine or cording

Awl, skewer or hole punch (optional)

Button with large holes

INSTRUCTIONS

Cut out the cereal box to create the cover for the journal. You can make it as large or as small as you want to, but my kids like to use one whole side of a cereal box, so they can use regular computer or grid paper in their journal. Fold it in half so that the blank cardboard side is facing out. Glue a piece of scrapbook or wrapping paper to both the inside and outside to make a pretty lining and cover. Trim any excess paper.

Use the needle and twine to sew the button onto what will be the front of the journal. Leave about 12 inches (30 cm) of twine hanging. You'll use that to wrap around the journal and then around the button to close it.

My kids like to use 20 to 25 sheets of computer paper or grid paper for the pages of their journals. You can make yours as full as you'd like. Lay the paper in the inside of the journal (if it is bigger than the cover, you'll need to trim it so that it is about ¼ inch [6 mm] smaller than the cover on all sides).

Using the needle and twine, stitch the paper to the cover down the spine. My kids and I like to use an awl—which is a pointy tool that's used to poke holes for crafting—to make three holes in the spine of the journal first to make it easier to poke the needles through and sew it all together. You can use a skewer or even a hole punch if you don't have an awl. Just poke a hole near the top, middle and bottom of the journal's spine.

Want it to come together even easier? Poke holes in the center of the papers, too! Then, sew it all together, and you have the most amazing nature journal ever! We love experimenting with new colors and papers to make ours!

(continued)

Now, tuck your journal, some colored pencils (watercolor pencils are awesome), pencils, a portable sharpener, binoculars, magnifying glass, small containers for collecting specimens, old spoons or a small shovel for digging in the dirt, and other things you might need in your explorations into a small backpack or tote bag. You'll always have your tools ready and waiting for you.

Head out to your yard, find a comfortable place to sit and draw or write what you see. It's so fun to look back on nature and science journals like this—you can see all of the adventures you've been on! Throughout the book, I mention writing something down in your journal—this is the journal I'm talking about! Keep it with you, and document all of your amazing explorations. You'll treasure it always!

FUN FACT: Henry David Thoreau is the author of some of the most famous nature journals of all time. They were full of personal reflections, drawings and observations. Often, there was a combination like this reflective observation, "I saw a bird flying across the street with so long a strip of cloth, or the like, the other day, and so slowly that at first I thought it was a little boy's kite with a long tail." I wonder what kinds of cool observations you'll make in your journal!

SUPER SIMPLE BUG BOXES

GREAT BACKYARD EXPLORERS GET TO KNOW THE PLANTS AND ANIMALS THEY'RE STUDYING BY OBSERVING THEM CLOSELY. YOU'LL NEED TO CATCH CRITTERS AND DIG THINGS UP. AND YOU'LL NEED PLACES TO KEEP THEM TEMPORARILY, WHEN THEY'RE NOT CRAWLING UP AND DOWN YOUR ARM!

THERE ARE LOTS OF DIFFERENT BUG BOXES AVAILABLE IN STORES EVERYWHERE. MY KIDS PICK OUT SEVERAL LITTLE PLASTIC BUG BOXES FROM THE DISCOUNT STORE EVERY SPRING. BUT WE ALSO LOVE MAKING OUR OWN FROM RECYCLABLES AROUND THE HOUSE—TAKE A LOOK IN YOUR RECYCLE BIN AND SEE WHAT YOU CAN REPURPOSE TO BE A GREAT BUG HOUSE!

MATERIALS

Small containers, such as plastic berry crates, canning jars with lids and glass pickle or sauce jars

Colored duct tape

A nail, awl, craft knife or another sharp tool

INSTRUCTIONS

The plastic containers that blueberries and strawberries come in can make great homes for little backyard creatures. Simply snap them closed and seal the edges with decorated duct tape!

Then, have an adult help you cut a rectangle-shaped opening in the top with a nail, awl, craft knife or other sharp tool so you can put your bug into their fantastically cool temporary home. You can use more duct tape to make a hinge on the plastic rectangle you cut out, so you can open and close the bug box easily. It's like a bug palace!

For a simpler bug home, have a grown up drill holes in the lids of leftover food jars. Clean them out really well, get outside and find a critter, put some dirt and plants in the bottom, and let your bug friend enjoy its new digs.

MORE FUN: Make a portable bug box necklace. The next time you go to the grocery store with your parents, get something out of one of the toy vending machines for a quarter or two, and save the plastic container. Have an adult drill small air holes in the lid, and a bigger hole in the middle of it. Tie a necklace cord with a big knot through the middle hole. Put a little ladybug friend in the toy container and snap the lid on. Wear your friend around on your adventures for a day, then let it go free in the evening. Maybe you can even write a story about your little bug friend's adventures in your nature journal to remember the day you had together!

THE BEST BUG NET EVER

YOU HAVE BOXES AND CONTAINERS, BUT SOME OF THOSE QUICKER CRITTERS MIGHT BE A BIT MORE CHALLENGING FOR YOU TO CATCH. HAVE YOU EVER TRIED TO CATCH A BUTTERFLY WITH JUST YOUR HANDS? NOT TOO EASY, IS IT? A NET CAN HELP.

IT'S SUPER EASY TO MAKE THE PERFECT BUG CATCHING NET AT HOME WITH THINGS YOU LIKELY ALREADY HAVE ON HAND. YOU MAY NEED TO RUN TO THE STORE WITH AN ADULT TO GRAB AN EMBROIDERY HOOP. BUT THOSE ARE INEXPENSIVE AND EASY TO FIND.

READY? LET'S GET STARTED!

MATERIALS

Small embroidery hoop (wooden or plastic)

Mesh produce bag or leftover fabric (tulle or muslin works best)

Scissors (optional)

Craft wire

Stick or wooden dowel

Duct tape

INSTRUCTIONS

Got your materials? Great. Now head outside to your backyard. Let's go!

First, loosen the screw on the small embroidery hoop and slide out the smaller ring. Simple—now you've got two rings. Take the produce bag or fabric (we used tulle we had left over from a costume we once made) and wrap the ends over the small ring.

Slip the small, fabric or bag covered ring back into the outer ring and tighten up the screw. The fabric should form a pouch now, with the embroidery hoop holding it open. It's a net with no handle! You're almost there! If there is any excess fabric or mesh hanging over the edge once it's tightened, feel free to trim it close with a pair of scissors.

Use the colored wire to attach the stick or dowel to your net tightly. We wrapped ours around the hoop, poking it through the holes in the tulle, then around and down along the stick. It holds well (and lasts longer) if you extend down the stick a bit with the wire.

Finally, use the duct tape to cover up any sharp points sticking out, and to cover the wire completely. Since we used decorative duct tape, we wrapped ours all the way down the handle of our bug net. We love how it turned out!

You're all set to catch flying insects like butterflies without using your hands! Head outside and have fun!

FUNNIES: WHY DID THE BOY THROW THE BUTTER OUT THE WINDOW?
TO SEE A BUTTERFLY!

EPIC MIRROR BOX FOR OBSERVING NATURE

WHILE A MIRROR BOX ISN'T NECESSARY FOR CATCHING AND OBSERVING ANYTHING, IT CAN MAKE IT AN EVEN COOLER EXPERIENCE. WITH A MIRROR BOX, YOU'RE ABLE TO SEE ALL THE DIFFERENT SIDES OF A CRITTER AT THE SAME TIME. AWESOME!

AND THIS ONE IS SUPER SIMPLE TO MAKE—ESPECIALLY IF YOU HAVE METALLIC SCRAPBOOKING PAPER LEFTOVER FROM FANCY HOLIDAY CARDS OR A SIMILAR PROJECT. A GOOD QUALITY ALUMINUM FOIL MIGHT WORK, TOO. LET'S GO!

MATERIALS

Quart or half gallon cardboard milk carton

Scissors

Silver metallic (mirror-like) scrapbooking paper or metallic tape

Transparent tape

INSTRUCTIONS

Are you ready? This one's a little technical—but so, so cool. Make sure you read the directions carefully. It will be totally worth it!

Have an adult help you cut the milk carton in half across the middle so you have the bottom box-like portion and the top of the carton. You'll only need the bottom part for this activity, so go ahead and put the top part in the recycling bin.

It's easier to put the mirror tape or paper on a flat surface, so cut along the sides of the bottom half of your carton, down towards the bottom. Flatten it into one piece.

Tape your silver mirror-like paper to the inside of the flattened carton securely. Then, fold the sides back up and tape the carton together again.

Hooray! You did it!

Bring this outside with you so the next time you catch a ladybug, ant, grasshopper or another small critter, you can put it gently in your mirror box.

Isn't it amazing to see its movement from all angles? I just love being able to see an insect's underside as I look down on it.

MORE FUN: Want to try catching more insects to check out in your mirror box or bug box? Grab a large, light-colored sheet (white works best) and spread it out under a tree. Have an adult help you shake the branches really hard for a minute or two. Explore the sheet to see what insects, caterpillars, spiders and other creatures you had hanging out in your yard. Then, put a couple of them into one of the bug boxes you already made from the directions on page 15, and check them out one by one in your epic mirror box.

BACKYARD ENTOMOLOGY

(EN-[T]E-MÄ-LE-JĒ)

BEETLES, BUGS AND MORE

Do you like catching butterflies in the yard? Or do you prefer ladybugs or spiders? Maybe you like them all . . . I know I do! Entomology is the study of insects, and most entomologists specialize in one type of insect or arachnid.

This chapter is my favorite (shhh! don't tell anyone!) because you get to catch *real* bugs, worms, insects and larvae to observe and experiment with. It's seriously cool to feel the scratchy feet of a bess bug as it walks up your arm, or the cool sliminess of a worm flopping around in the palm of your hand.

To be sure that you keep them safe—whether you're outside checking out roly poly bugs, worms, butterflies or caterpillars—you need to have gentle tools to catch and keep them.

When you're making ground traps like the one on page 22, or finding roly poly bugs to observe and experiment with, it's important to be careful with them.

When you play, experiment and explore with nature, you need to be a good steward, and keep living things safe. Respect them and their natural habitats, and you'll be able to enjoy them for a long, long time.

Are you ready to go on a backyard bug safari and be an entomologist? I can't wait to explore with you. Grab your sense of adventure, your nature journal and let's go!

FUN FACT: Insects can be found on all seven continents—even Antarctica! The Antarctic midge (*Belgica antarctica*) is a purplish-black insect that can absorb heat from the sun, live two years in its larval form, and go without oxygen for up to four weeks! Its larvae survive by eating moss, microorganisms and a terrestrial (land) algae called *Prasiola crispa*. The adults only live up to 10 days—long enough to mate and lay eggs. I wonder what the strangest insect is that YOU have in your backyard? Get out there and find out!

THE EASIEST GROUND BUG TRAP YOU'LL EVER MAKE

CATCHING BUTTERFLIES AND OTHER FLYING INSECTS IS A LOT OF FUN, BUT THERE ARE SO MANY COOL CREATURES CREEPING AROUND YOUR YARD, TOO. WHAT ABOUT THE ONES NEAR THE GROUND? OR THE ONES THAT COME OUT AT NIGHT?

CAPTURING WORMS, CENTIPEDES AND OTHER GROUND CREATURES IS EASY WITH THIS TRAP MADE OUT OF RECYCLABLES. AND IT'S THE PERFECT ADDITION TO YOUR OUTDOOR BUG COLLECTING KIT!

MATERIALS

Small plastic cup or yogurt container without a lid

Larger plastic container or carton without a lid

Trowel or small shovel

Scissors

Large stone

Your Nature Journal (page 12)

Super Simple Bug Box (page 15)

INSTRUCTIONS

Before doing this activity, check with your parents. You'll need to dig a small hole in the yard or garden—or even under a bush—so you can catch insects overnight. It only needs to be big enough to fit the small container, and you can fill it back in once you've caught some bugs, but you should get permission first.

Once you're ready, clean and dry both the large and small containers really well.

Dig that hole we chatted about—and the one you already got permission to dig—and drop the small cup or yogurt container into it so that the container's opening is level with the ground.

Pack the dirt tightly around it.

Now, you're going to use the larger container to protect the smaller one in case it rains. It'll be a cover for the smaller container, but you still need insects to be able to fall into the hole you dug. To make sure they can get in, but the hole stays protected, cut doors into the top lip of the larger container. When you flip the container upside down over the smaller one, the doors will give insects easy access to the trap.

Got that? Great! Now, put a stone on top of the roof to weigh it down, and leave it alone until the next day.

I know . . . waiting is always the toughest part. While you're waiting, you can draw a picture in your nature journal of what your trap looks like before any bugs fall in.

In the morning, head out to the backyard to see if any new friends decided to drop by for a visit. Scoop them into your bug box, or create a habitat for them so you can observe or try some of the activities in this chapter with them. When you check your bug trap, make sure you take a minute to identify the bugs you caught. Use an insect field guide or the Internet to figure out the identification of any unfamiliar bugs to make sure they are all safe to handle. If there are any that you can't identify, let them go without touching them. You don't want to take a chance that an unfamiliar insect could harm you. Only experiment with familiar bugs.

Make sure that you put the little creepy-crawlies back where they belong once you're done observing them.

FUN FACT: Instead of closed circulatory systems like humans, insects have an open system where their "blood," called hemolymph, flows through the body cavity, bathing the organs. Hemolymph is usually clear, but can be yellow or greenish too. The heart is chambered and runs along an insect's back, sending the hemolymph up towards the head, then sloshing back into the body. Can you imagine that? It probably feels strange to have all that fluid sloshing around inside one's body. When you catch some insects in your ground trap, hold them up to the light to see if you can observe evidence of their circulatory systems in action.

ROLY POLY INVESTIGATIONS

HAVE YOU EVER PICKED UP A STONE AND TAKEN A PEEK UNDERNEATH?

Try it! If you don't have a stone in your yard, you can roll over a log, brick or some other heavy thing that's been sitting for a while with dirt underneath. There's a hidden world of creepy crawlies that make their homes where you can't easily see them. Like right under your feet!

One type of bug you might find under that stone (or a fallen log) is the roly poly (*Armadillidiidae*). Roly poly bugs are super common, though you might have heard them called potato bugs, pill bugs or sow bugs. They're all the same bug—small, oval-shaped, with a brownish or gray shell called an exoskeleton. Roly poly bugs have seven sets of legs and two sets of antennae. Believe it or not, these little bugs aren't bugs at all. They're actually crustaceans just like lobsters and crabs.

Can you believe that? You've got crustaceans living in your yard!

Roly poly bugs are harmless to touch, pick up and let crawl along your hands and arms, and the perfect size to watch and learn from. Go ahead—give it a try. Their little legs feel feathery soft and tickle a bit as they scoot across your skin.

Grab a clear container with a vented lid or one of those bug boxes you made from recyclables on page 15, and head outside to find a big stone, brick or log. Roll it over and gently pick up a few roly poly bugs. Put them and a bit of soil in your container to serve as a temporary habitat so they're comfortable while you're learning from them.

The study of animal behavior is called ethology. Roly poly bugs are perfect for studying how an animal reacts in different situations. Try the investigations in this section to determine the reason you find roly poly bugs under logs and rocks.

Grab your nature journal and the materials for each activity on the next few pages! You want to be just like a real scientist, right? Scientists document all that they do so they can do it all over again. Keep track of what you do throughout the book in that special journal you made on page 12.

Before you start experimenting with roly poly bugs, though, draw the place where you found them so you can return them to their home when your experiments are done.

FUNNIES: WHAT DO YOU CALL A HOCKEY-PLAYING ROLY POLY BUG?

A GOALIE POLY!

COOL CRITTER CHOICE CONTAINER

WHEN YOU'RE TESTING AN ANIMAL'S BEHAVIOR, YOU NEED TO USE A TESTING VESSEL THAT GIVES THE ANIMAL A WAY TO GET FROM ONE CHOICE TO ANOTHER.

WHILE EXPLORING ROLY POLY BUGS, YOU'RE GOING TO TEST THEIR PREFERENCES BETWEEN SEVERAL DIFFERENT OPPOSITE CHOICES (LIGHT/DARK, WET/DRY, SWEET/SALTY, ETC.). THIS COOL CRITTER CHOICE CONTAINER MAKES CHOOSING THEIR FAVORITES EASY FOR YOUR CRUSTACEAN FRIENDS!

IT'S GOING TO BE SO MUCH FUN!

MATERIALS

Toilet paper or paper towel roll, or other tube of similar size

Two same-sized clear plastic containers or cups

Marker

Scissors

Electrical, duct or masking tape

INSTRUCTIONS

Put the tube against the side of one of the cups, as near to the bottom as you can, and trace around it with the marker. Do that again on the other cup. Get an adult to help you use the scissors to cut out each of the circles, making a tube-sized hole in each cup.

Tape the tube between the openings, joining the two cups together. Seal the openings completely by taping both the inside and the outside.

Now your roly poly bugs—and any critters you catch for the activities in this book—will be able to travel from one cup to the other through the tube. Get ready to try out some experiments now! You're going to love this next part!

FUN FACT: Roly poly mamas carry their eggs around with them in a special pouch called a marsupium. When they first hatch, roly poly babies hang out in the pouch for a few days before heading out into the world to explore. That's one of the reasons it's so important to put your roly poly bugs back exactly where you found them when you're done observing them—they want to be with their family just like you do!

WET BUGS, DRY BUGS

ROLY POLY BUG EXPERIMENT ONE

WHAT DO YOU THINK? WILL THE ROLY POLY BUGS PREFER THE SIDE OF THE CONTAINER THAT HAS THE DAMP PAPER TOWEL? OR WILL THEY PREFER THE DRY SIDE? IN THIS SIMPLE EXPERIMENT, YOU'LL TEST YOUR HYPOTHESIS—OR SCIENTIFIC GUESS—AND SEE WHAT HAPPENS WHEN YOU GIVE ROLY POLY BUGS A CHOICE.

SO, GRAB YOUR ROLY POLY BUGS AND HEAD OUT IN THE YARD WITH YOUR CHOICE CONTAINER, FIND A COZY SPOT IN THE GRASS AND SEE WHAT THEY DO!

MATERIALS

Your Cool Critter Choice Container (page 26)

Paper towel

Spray bottle of water

Your Nature Journal (page 12)

INSTRUCTIONS

Do you have a table in your yard? We love doing these activities on the picnic table or sprawling down on the grass. Remember to get outside and build your brain!

Get your choice container ready for the experiment. Put a paper towel flat on the bottom of one side of the container and mist it with the spray bottle so that it is damp. Leave the other side dry.

Do you remember what a hypothesis is? It's an educated guess, basically. Scientists have an idea about what's going to happen when they try out an experiment, so they write it down then see what really happens. They use their results to design new and better hypotheses and experiments, learning more and more about their world.

You can too!

Which side do you think your roly poly bugs will prefer? Make your hypothesis by writing (or drawing) it in your nature journal.

Set half of your roly poly bugs in the wet side of the container and the other half in the dry side.

Watch your roly poly bugs. What are they doing? Jot down what you're seeing so you can look back in your nature journal later and remember the experiment.

To give them a chance to show you which conditions they really prefer, leave them alone for five minutes. Take a look at the clock, and write down the time you got started.

While you're waiting for your five minutes to go by, make a simple chart in your nature journal. Have three columns and seven rows. In the top box of the first column write Time Elapsed. In the top box of the second column write Wet. Write Dry in the top box of the third column. Under the Time Elapsed column, write 5 Minutes, 10 Minutes, 15 Minutes, 20 Minutes, 25 Minutes and 30 Minutes. It will look like this:

TIME ELAPSED	WET	DRY
5 Minutes		
10 Minutes		
15 Minutes		
20 Minutes		
25 Minutes		
30 Minutes		

Once five minutes have passed, check to see how many roly poly bugs are in each side of the choice container. Write the number under the correct column. Recheck the choice container every five minutes for a half an hour to give your roly poly bugs enough time to explore.

Once a half an hour has elapsed, write down your final count and then look over the results. Was your hypothesis correct? Why do you think this was the case? What surprised you? Write down and sketch your observations and conclusions. Then transfer your roly poly bugs back into their holding container to rest up for the next activity. Even crustaceans need a break!

MORE FUN: If you want something fun to do while you wait, and if you're the dancing type, my kids love the song Roly Poly by Roger Day. You can listen to it on YouTube and dance around while the roly poly bugs make their choices.

LIGHT BUGS, DARK BUGS
ROLY POLY BUG EXPERIMENT TWO

YOU'VE HAD THE CHANCE TO CHECK OUT HOW THE ROLY POLY BUGS BEHAVE WHEN GIVEN ONE CHOICE—HOW DO YOU THINK THEY'LL BEHAVE THIS TIME? WILL THEY PREFER THE DARK SIDE OR THE LIGHT SIDE? I CAN'T WAIT TO FIND OUT! LET'S GET TO IT!

MATERIALS

Your Cool Critter Choice Container (page 26)

Dark colored paper

Tape

Your Nature Journal (page 12)

INSTRUCTIONS

You're going to set up your experiment in the same way you did with experiment one from page 28, except instead of putting a damp paper towel inside of the choice container, you'll completely cover all but the bottom of one of the sides with your dark colored paper and tape. The idea is to make one side open to the light and the other dark. You'll need to leave a part of the paper open until you put your roly poly bugs in.

On a new page in your nature journal, record your hypothesis for this experiment. Will the roly poly bugs prefer the dark side or the light side of the choice container?

Then, make a similar table to the one on page 29, but instead of labeling the columns Wet and Dry, you'll label them Dark and Light. Follow the same steps you did before—checking and recording every five minutes, and then drawing your conclusion.

TIME ELAPSED	DARK	LIGHT
5 Minutes		
10 Minutes		
15 Minutes		
20 Minutes		
25 Minutes		
30 Minutes		

What happened? Why? Based on what you learned in experiments one and two together, what can you conclude about a roly poly bug's preferred habitat? Hint: think, too, about where you found them in your yard.

Roly poly bugs like habitats that are dark and damp, which is why the underside of a log or stone is perfect for them. You can find roly poly bugs around the world in grasslands, forests, rainforests—anywhere that's damp. They need to stay moist because they breathe through gill-like membranes at the base of their abdomens.

Female roly poly bugs hold up to two dozen eggs in a liquid-filled brood pouch until they're ready to hatch. Can you imagine having one or two dozen eggs sloshing around in a pouch attached to you? Strange!

Once the babies hatch, both the female and the male roly poly bugs raise their family together, often living out their lives in the burrow, only leaving to scout for food.

The whole family works hard to gather food and to clean out their waste to keep their burrow clean. Do you help YOUR parents keep your house clean like a good roly poly does? Next time you do your chores, tell your mom that you're just being a good roly poly!

FUNNIES: WHAT DO YOU CALL A ROLY POLY IN CHURCH?
A HOLY POLY!

ANT EXPLORATIONS

I BET YOU THINK YOU KNOW ALL ABOUT ANTS (FORMICIDAE), RIGHT?

They're everywhere, and you probably see them all the time—in your yard, on the sidewalk or even (yikes!) in your kitchen.

You might not know everything about them, though. Check this out. . . .

Ants are very social insects that can have up to thousands of busy ants in their colonies, each doing the unique job for which they were made. (So when you see an ant in the house, it's probably not the only one there!)

All colonies have a queen ant whose only job is to lay eggs. Male ants have the task of mating with the queen, and they have a very short life span. The hardest working, and longest living ants are the female workers. They build the tunnels in the colony, hunt for food, tend the eggs and protect the queen. Hmmm. Sounds kind of like my job as the mom of four kids!

Ants are pretty neat to watch. Head outside with your nature journal and see if you can find some. Settle down near where they're working and watch what they do. Draw a picture in your nature journal and maybe write a few questions or observations down. Maybe you'll even be lucky enough to find an anthill to draw!

Most ants build a system of tunnels under a mound. The tunnels connect chambers—each used for specific purposes. Some chambers are where the workers rest. Others serve as nurseries. Still others are storage chambers for food.

Now, try the following activities to learn more about these fascinating insects. But be careful! Some ants do bite, so it's best if you don't handle ants directly. When I do an activity that · requires moving ants to a habitat or viewing container, I scoop them with a small shovel, and then put them right into a container.

FUN FACT: Ants can carry twenty times their own body weight—that would be like you carrying a car!

BUSY BUSY ANTS
ANT EXPERIMENT ONE

USUALLY SCOUTS FROM ANT COLONIES WILL HEAD OUT TO HUNT FOR FOOD, AND THEN HEAD BACK TO THE COLONY TO TELL OTHERS. THEY LEAVE A SCENT TRAIL OF PHEROMONES TO MARK THE PATH BACK TO THE FOOD SOURCE SO THEY CAN FIND THEIR WAY BACK AND LEAD OTHERS ALONG THE PATH.

SOMETIMES IT'S FUN TO SEE IF YOU CAN CONFUSE THE CRITTERS THAT DO THEIR WORK IN YOUR YARD. IF ANTS LEAVE PHEROMONE TRAILS TO FIND THEIR WAY BETWEEN HOME AND FOOD, WHAT MIGHT HAPPEN IF THEY SUDDENLY CAN'T FIND THEIR ORIGINAL TRAIL? IT'S TIME TO PLAY AROUND WITH AN ANT FAMILY TO FIND OUT!

MATERIALS

Your Nature Journal (page 12)

Ripe fruit or another sugary treat for bait

A piece of wood, a book or some building blocks

INSTRUCTIONS

Take your nature journal outside and search for an ant colony. The best place to find ants is in the dirt or sandy soil. Observe the ants for a bit, then see if you can confuse them. Place the food treat a few inches (6 or 7 cm) away from the ant hill, and watch what happens.

How long does it take for the ants to find the sweet treat? In your journal draw the path the ants took to find the bait, and make a note about approximately how long it took them to get there.

What happened?

What do you think will happen if you put an obstruction, or something to block them, in the way of that scent-marked path? Will the ants become confused? Will they eventually find their way back to the food source along another path?

Write down your hypothesis in your journal and place your wood, book or block in the way of the ants' path. A hypothesis is a scientific guess you make based on what you know about the subject you're studying. Draw where you put the obstruction in your journal, and take notes about what you see the ants do.

Usually, it will take the ants a few minutes of confusion before they'll find their way again and mark a new pheromone-scented path. Is that what you observed? Don't forget to write down your observations and conclusions in your journal.

> **MORE FUN:** Set a new piece of food down, and time how long it takes for the ants to find the new bait. Then, set another obstruction in the ants' path, and time how long it takes them to find their way around the obstruction. You can try this again and again with different foods to see if the type of bait makes a difference.

HUNGRY, HUNGRY ANTS
ANT EXPERIMENT TWO

NOW THAT YOU KNOW HOW ANTS FIND FOOD AND COMMUNICATE WITH ONE ANOTHER, DO YOU WONDER IF THEY PREFER ONE TYPE OVER ANOTHER? SCIENTISTS ASK QUESTIONS LIKE THIS ALL THE TIME.

I THINK IT'S INCREDIBLE HOW MANY THINGS YOU CAN DO AND LEARN WITHOUT EVER LEAVING YOUR OWN BACKYARD. HEAD BACK OUTSIDE TO THE ANTHILL WITH YOUR FOOD AND NATURE JOURNAL. IT'S TIME TO LEARN MORE ABOUT THE HABITS OF YOUR BACKYARD ANT FRIENDS.

MATERIALS

Four different types of food (for example: a crushed up pretzel, a gummy candy cut up, honey and some rice)

Your Nature Journal (page 12)

INSTRUCTIONS

Set out your four food choices near the anthill. Make sure that each food type is about equidistant (the same distance) from the ant colony.

Now watch and observe.

Which food type do you think the ants will prefer? Which will they find faster? Will they try to take all of the food types back to the colony? Or will they choose to focus on just one type? Write down your hypotheses in your journal.

What happened? Did the ants like the sweeter foods better? Why do you think the ants preferred the foods they did? Most insects are attracted to sugary foods because they provide quick energy. Write what happened and your conclusions in your nature journal.

FUNNIES: WHICH INSECTS ARE THE BEST BUILDERS?
CARPENTER ANTS!

AWESOME ANT HOTEL

YOU'VE PROBABLY SEEN THE ANT FARMS THAT YOU CAN BUY IN THE STORES. THEY COME WITH SAND OR GEL AND A COUPON TO SEND AWAY FOR A VIAL OF ANTS. HERE'S YOUR CHANCE TO MAKE ONE THAT'S MORE NATURAL AND FUN TO VIEW. SERIOUSLY—THIS AWESOME ANT HABITAT WILL MAKE THE ANTS THAT HAVE TO LIVE IN THE YARD ENVIOUS! (OKAY . . . MAYBE NOT, BUT THE ANTS THAT DO LIVE IN IT WILL LOVE IT!)

MATERIALS

2 (2-liter) soda bottles

1 (20-ounce [591-ml]) soda bottle

Quick-set epoxy or glue

Utility knife (used with adult supervision)

Funnel

Shipping tape

Soil

Duct tape or an inexpensive tornado tube

Small patch of grass, rocks, twigs, etc.

Cotton balls

Ants (get these last after reading through the instructions and putting together your habitat)

Your Nature Journal (page 12)

INSTRUCTIONS

Make sure you get an adult to help you with this activity as you'll be using a razor-sharp utility knife and super strong epoxy or glue, and build this outside so you can make as big a mess as you need to.

First, take the labels off of each of the bottles and clean them out completely.

Then, have an adult help you use the utility knife to cut the bottom off of both 2-liter bottles along the ridge that's about 2 inches (5 cm) up. To make it easier, you can use the utility knife to make the first cut, and then use a pair of scissors to finish.

Once you have both bottoms cut off of the two 2-liter bottles, use the epoxy or glue to attach the small bottle (with its lid in place) to the inside of one of the bottoms you cut off. Make sure it's secured. This smaller bottle takes up the space in the middle of the ant farm bottle so that when your little workers begin to build a colony, they'll do it against the outer wall so you can see their tunnels.

Let it dry completely—this might take a while, so check the instructions on the epoxy bottle before you get started.

When the epoxy, or glue, is dried, put the top back onto that bottom and seal the seam with epoxy. Take your time on this step. You want to make sure that the seam is completely sealed so that no dirt (or ants!) comes out. It might take several applications to get this seal. Let the epoxy or glue set completely in between applications. Once the epoxy is set, you can blow gently into the top of the 2-liter bottle and feel along the seam to see if air escapes anywhere.

This is the part where you have to just be patient. It's going to feel tedious to seal the bottle, then reseal it, again and again, but it's totally worth it—trust me. This ant hotel is really great.

Now that you have the bottom of your new ant habitat in place, use the funnel to add soil. If it's possible, find an ant colony outside in your yard (you'll need them to populate the habitat in the end anyway). Use soil from near the natural ant colony in your yard. Just gently fill the bottle up using your funnel. Fill it completely to the top because you'll want the ants to be able to dig straight down once you add the foraging area on top of their habitat.

(continued)

> NOTE: If you can't find an ant colony in your yard, relax. Just use any dirt or soil from your yard to get set up. You can hunt around your neighborhood once your habitat is ready. There are ants to be found just about anywhere—and there are even a few places you can order them from if you aren't having luck finding a colony in your yard. Check out the More Resources section on page 201. You'll see a link there to a webpage that has lots of links to find extra things—like ants—to make your backyard nature science explorations epic.

Now, take the second 2-liter bottle. If you bought a tornado tube to use in this activity, connect the two bottles by screwing them together. If not—no big deal! Duct tape works wonders. Grab some fun-colored duct tape and connect the two bottles by taping the openings together tightly. When I did this, I wanted to make sure that there were no openings, so I used a little bit of the epoxy to secure the seam between the two bottles, and then, once it set, I taped the duct tape around the two bottle tops.

In the top area, you'll create a foraging zone for your ants so they have all they need to survive in their new habitat. First, pour more soil in, pushing it down so there is a continuous flow of the soil from the top bottle to the bottom one. Fill it about half way. Then, plant the grass patch in the top and mist it because your ants will prefer moist soil. You can add some rocks or sticks to decorate the area further.

Finally, take the remaining bottle bottom, and tuck it, bump side down, into the top of your foraging area, creating a sealed habitat. If you're worried that the ants will escape, you can cut a quarter-sized hole in the bottom of the "lid" and tuck a dry cotton ball into it and attach the lid to the bottle with packing tape. This will allow air to flow into the habitat, but block the ants from escaping.

Add the ants (try to find a queen if you can) and a tiny amount of the food you discovered that they prefer in the experiment from page 35. Mist your habitat about once a week. Feed them regularly too, but don't add too much food at once. You don't want the food to have a chance to mold and contaminate your ant habitat. If you notice food sitting around, uneaten, it probably means that you're feeding them too much. Just scoop out the uneaten food and feed them less often.

Enjoy observing your ant colony. Draw what it looks like now in your nature journal, and check back, drawing what you see every few days.

> MORE FUN: Ants prefer the dark, so if you want to encourage them to build their tunnels and do their work right up against the walls of their habitat so you can see it more easily, cover the habitat in dark black construction paper and only check it every few days so they feel like they're really in the dark.

WARM ANT, COOL ANT

ANT EXPERIMENT THREE

DO YOU SEE MANY ANTS DURING THE COLDER MONTHS OF THE YEAR? WHY? LET'S SEE HOW TEMPERATURE AFFECTS OUR ANT FRIENDS. IT'S A SUPER SIMPLE ACTIVITY—AND REALLY COOL. . . . (GET IT?)

MATERIALS

Small shovel

Bug Box (page 15) or a clean, clear food container with a lid

Your Nature Journal (page 12)

INSTRUCTIONS

Scoop up some ants from outside, using a small shovel, into your bug box or a see-through container. Be careful not to touch them in case they are a type that bites or stings.

Grab your nature journal and draw your container and the ants inside it. Make observations. Remember, these are your observations, so they are anecdotal, which means what you think you're seeing. You don't need to time their movements, just describe them. What are they doing? How quickly are they moving around? Are they trying to get out of the container? Do they look like they're communicating with one another? How?

Once you've written out some observations, put your container of ants into the refrigerator for ten minutes.

What do you think will happen? Write your hypothesis in your journal. Your hypothesis should answer the questions—How do you think the cold will affect the ants and why do you think that will happen.

When you remove the ant container from the refrigerator, sit and watch them for a bit. How are they acting differently than before? Describe their movements in your journal. Was your hypothesis correct? Why do you think the ants are now behaving this way?

Ants are pretty interesting to observe. They're great over-winterers. During the fall, as colder temperatures approach, they eat more food, and put on extra fat stores.

When the temperatures drop, ants become sluggish and burrow down into their colony, huddling together around their queen to protect her. Because they're not really moving around, the openings of their burrows close up, further insulating them.

As warmer temperatures arrive in the spring, the ants warm up and begin to stir. They start clearing their tunnels and opening back up their entrances. They go out in search of food, and when they find it the worker ants eat their fill, then go back to let the others know about it, starting the cycle of gathering food, mating and tending the queen and the young all over again.

FUN FACT: A queen ant in Idaho was the oldest ant on record—she lived for 30 years! Can you imagine that? How old do you think the ants that you caught are? I'll bet they're not 30!

FUN WITH BEETLES

It's pretty hard to venture anywhere outside without coming across a bunch of different types of beetles. Did you know that there are over 350,000 species of beetles in the world with over 12,000 of them living in the United States?

AREN'T THOSE CRAZY-HIGH NUMBERS?

No wonder there are always ladybugs, fireflies, borers, weevils and more every time we head outside. Some are harmful—like the emerald ash borer—which has done tremendous damage to ash trees in the eastern United States. Some, like the ladybug, are helpful and eat harmful pests that would otherwise destroy our gardens and crops.

Adult beetles have two sets of wings. One set acts as a hard outer shell, protecting the more fragile flying wings that hide underneath.

There are many, many field guides available to help you identify backyard beetles in your area. I highly recommend getting one, or finding one online. You can see some of my suggestions in the resources section in the back of the book (page 201).

Start exploring with some of the most easy-to-identify beetles you're likely to see outside in your yard throughout the spring and summer. You'll see which foods they like, which colors they prefer and more! Have fun!

FUN FACT: There are over 350,000 types of beetles that have been discovered in the world, but scientists believe there are many more that haven't been discovered yet. There could be as many as 3 million! Can you even imagine 3 million different types of beetles? That's a lot of beetles to discover!

RED FLOWER, BLUE FLOWER
LADYBUG EXPERIMENT ONE

I OFTEN WONDER ABOUT LADYBUGS (COCCINELLIDAE) AND OTHER CRITTERS IN THE YARD WHEN I'M SITTING OUTSIDE WATCHING. DO YOU? WHEN I'M SEEING LADYBUGS IN THE GARDEN, FOR EXAMPLE, I OFTEN WONDER IF THEY HAVE A PREFERENCE ABOUT THE COLORS OF THE PLANTS AND FLOWERS I PLANT IN THERE. IN THIS ACTIVITY, WE'LL SEE IF WE CAN GET TO THE BOTTOM OF THAT QUESTION.

CHECK THIS OUT, AND LET ME KNOW WHAT RESULTS YOU GET BECAUSE WE'VE HAD MIXED RESULTS EACH TIME WE'VE TRIED THIS OUT. YOU CAN FIND MY CONTACT INFORMATION IN THE ABOUT THE AUTHOR SECTION (PAGE 203).

MATERIALS

Several flowers in different colors

Ladybugs in a container

Your Nature Journal (page 12)

A large solid-colored bedsheet (optional)

INSTRUCTIONS

Go to a nice open area in your yard or driveway. If you're using a sheet, spread it out and set the flowers in the middle, a few inches (6 or 7 cm) apart from one another.

Let your ladybugs loose near the flowers and have a seat nearby to observe them, while documenting your observations in your nature journal. My kids love sketching the behavior of little creatures like ladybugs. Draw the flowers and where you set your beetles down, and then write quick notes about what they're doing.

Did you make a hypothesis? Which flower color did you think they'd prefer? Why? Are you noticing that the ladybugs are behaving as you predicted? Or are they doing something different? What are your theories about their behavior?

We love doing this activity. When the kids sit still for long enough, ladybugs land on them and crawl around, tickling their arms and legs. Have you ever caught a ladybug and let it wander around on your hand?

Ladybugs eat tiny insects called aphids. Those aphids love garden plants like tomatoes and flowers like nasturtium. They also eat other small insects like mites and whiteflies. To supplement their carbohydrate needs and give them a quick burst of energy if the insect population is down, ladybugs can also eat pollen and nectar from flowers.

One of my theories is that the type of flower is more important to ladybugs than color. I think they prefer flowers that have abundant pollen and nectar, and might also house aphids. I can't wait to hear about your experience.

> MORE FUN: Let your ladybugs go in the garden when you're done experimenting with them. They'll eat all those pesky little bugs that damage your flowers and vegetables. They're great garden helpers.

LIGHTS OUT, LIGHTS ON
LADYBUG EXPERIMENT TWO

WHAT DO YOU THINK? WILL LADYBUGS REACT TO THE CHOICE BETWEEN LIGHT AND DARK IN THE SAME WAY THAT YOUR ROLY POLY BUGS DID? THINK ABOUT HOW LADYBUGS AND ROLY POLY BUGS ARE SIMILAR AND DIFFERENT FROM ONE ANOTHER. I WONDER IF THEY LIKE THE SAME CONDITIONS? . . . LET'S FIND OUT!

MATERIALS

Small container of ladybugs

Your Cool Critter Choice Container (page 26)

Your Nature Journal (page 12)

Clear plastic wrap

Dark construction paper

Tape

INSTRUCTIONS

Head outside and set up your choice container the same way you did for the roly poly activity on page 30, taping dark construction paper on the outside of one side of the container, covering all but the bottom.

Create a table in your nature journal like you did on page 30 for the roly poly experiment.

TIME ELAPSED	DARK	LIGHT
5 Minutes		
10 Minutes		
15 Minutes		
20 Minutes		
25 Minutes		
30 Minutes		

Write down your hypothesis. Will the ladybugs prefer the light colored side or the dark colored one? Why do you think that?

Gently place your ladybugs into the container—half on each side—and cover the top of the light side with clear plastic wrap so the light shines in brightly.

Check on your ladybugs every five minutes, recording how many ladybugs are on each side. Once your half an hour has elapsed, look over your results. Are you surprised? Was your hypothesis correct? Why do you think this was the case?

FUNNIES: KNOCK KNOCK

WHO'S THERE?

LADYBUG

LADYBUG WHO?

LADY, GO BUG SOMEONE ELSE. I DON'T WANT TO BE BOTHERED!

SUPER SIMPLE LADYBUG HOUSE

NOW YOU KNOW HOW IMPORTANT THOSE LITTLE LADYBUG BEETLES ARE TO YOUR BACKYARD. THEY EAT THE PESTS THAT WOULD EAT YOUR TOMATO PLANTS OR KILL YOUR PRETTY FLOWERS. PLUS, THEY'RE VERY GENTLE AND FUN TO OBSERVE.

YOU CAN ATTRACT MORE TO YOUR YARD BY BUILDING A SIMPLE LADYBUG HOUSE TO GIVE THEM SHELTER AND A GREAT PLACE TO HIDE FROM PREDATORS. IT'S EASY! GIVE IT A TRY!

MATERIALS

Oatmeal (or other round) container with a lid

Paint

Paintbrush

Spray sealer

Utility knife

Wire

Your Nature Journal (page 12, optional)

INSTRUCTIONS

Find a spot outside that's perfect for painting, then decorate the outside of your oatmeal container. Cover it completely with a base coat of paint and then add fun details. Remember that ladybugs don't seem to have color preferences, but they are definitely attracted to the light. You may want to use light and bright paint colors to cover your oatmeal container.

Let it dry and then seal the container with the spray to help protect it from the weather.

Check with an adult before using the utility knife. Cut (or have help cutting) a small window slit on the top of your container. Then, cut a small door at the bottom of the container.

Poke a hole on either side of the oatmeal container and string the wire through it to create a hanger.

Hang your ladybug home from a tree near your garden or flower bed and watch for new ladybug families to come and set up their new home. If you want, you can use your nature journal to record how long it takes ladybugs to find your house and call it their own. Check on it each day, and draw or write about what you see.

MORE FUN: **You could kick-start your ladybug population by purchasing a bag of ladybugs. They're readily available at garden centers and online. Check out the resource section (page 201) for places I've used.**

FLICKERING FIREFLIES

Have you ever run around on late spring and summer evenings trying to catch fireflies (*Lampyridae*)? My kids always love trying to guess where the next flicker of light will come from and running to grab the gentle insects out of the air. When they're successful, they let them crawl around their arms, tickling them, before dropping the fireflies carefully into a bug box or jar where they observe them for a day before letting them go the next night.

DID YOU KNOW, THOUGH, THAT FIREFLIES AREN'T FLIES AT ALL?

They're actually beetles. There are over 2,000 species, or different types, of fireflies in the world. They're most easily found in warm, moist areas of the world.

Fireflies are bioluminescent animals. This means that they are able to make their own light. The light is made when a chemical reaction occurs in the insect's abdomen.

Fireflies light up for several reasons. They do it to warn predators that they are bad tasting. They do it to attract mates. And, if a firefly becomes agitated or disturbed, the frequency and intensity of their light increases.

FUN FACT: A firefly's light is extremely efficient—about ten times more energy efficient than the light bulb in your lamp at home! That means that it takes a lightning bug way less energy to make its light glow than it does for your lamp to light up. If scientists could figure out how to produce a glow as bright as a lightning bug, and as efficiently, we could light our homes up using very little electricity!

OBSERVING LIGHT PATTERNS AND TALKING TO FIREFLIES

DO YOU WONDER WHY FIREFLIES LIGHT UP? OR IF THERE IS A REASON THEY FLASH AND FLICKER IN THE WAYS THAT THEY DO?

SCIENTISTS BELIEVE THAT CERTAIN PATTERNS OF LIGHT FROM MALE FIREFLIES ATTRACT FEMALE FIREFLIES BETTER. AND, SCIENTISTS TAKE A LOT OF TIME STUDYING ANIMALS THEY ARE INTERESTED IN. HERE'S YOUR CHANCE TO BE A GREAT SCIENTIST, TOO! GATHER UP YOUR MATERIALS AND HEAD OUTSIDE TO OBSERVE AND TALK TO FIREFLIES. YOU'LL LEARN TO SPEAK THEIR LANGUAGE!

MATERIALS

Small flashlight (like a penlight)

Your Nature Journal (page 12)

INSTRUCTIONS

Head outside with your nature journal and find a quiet place to sit and watch the fireflies. Pay attention to the different patterns of lights in the sky and the patterns of lights in the grass. Jot down your observations or draw out the flight patterns of the lightning bugs you're observing. Remember that scientists keep track of what they're seeing in nature journals so that they can formulate conclusions about animal behavior.

Male fireflies flicker in the sky, trying to find a female mate flickering back in the grass. What do you notice about the light patterns? Are they quick? Short? Slow? Make notes about both the female and male beetles. Draw some of what you observe.

Now, pay special attention to the female fireflies in the grass or in low bushes. Choose one to watch closely.

Is she flashing long? Slowly? How many seconds go by between flashes? How many flashes does she make in a row? Once you think you have her pattern down, find a spot on the grass and try to attract a male firefly.

Hold your flashlight so it makes a small, beetle-sized point of light right on the grass. Turn it on and off, mimicking the flashes you observed the female firefly make. Keep doing this, calmly and patiently.

If you've figured out your neighborhood fireflies' "language," the males will be fooled and will start talking back to you by flashing and moving closer to you. Hopefully, one will land near your light.

Now you can talk to insects! You're amazing!

> FUN FACT: **Did you know that even firefly larvae glow? It's true! They're called glowworms, and the light warns predators that they'll taste bad.**

WARM BUGS, COOL BUGS
FIREFLY EXPERIMENT ONE

DID YOU KNOW THAT A LIGHTNING BUG'S GLOW WORKS SIMILARLY TO A GLOW STICK'S LIGHT? WHEN YOU BEND A GLOW STICK TO BREAK THE CHAMBER INSIDE, TWO CHEMICALS MIX TOGETHER AND GIVE OFF A GLOWING ENERGY WITH NO HEAT.

LIGHTNING BUGS HAVE DIFFERENT CHEMICALS, BUT THEY WORK IN THE SAME WAY, MIXING TOGETHER TO CAUSE A GLOW. YOU CAN USE GLOW STICKS TO HELP YOU LEARN MORE ABOUT LIGHTNING BUGS—LIKE HOW TEMPERATURE AFFECTS THEIR GLOW, FOR EXAMPLE. . . .

MATERIALS

Pitcher of ice water

Pitcher of hot water

Two identical glow sticks

Your Nature Journal (page 12)

INSTRUCTIONS

Do this experiment outside on a dark night.

First, get two pitchers filled with water—one should be really hot (but not boiling) and the other should be icy cold.

Take the two glow sticks and activate them however the packages tell you to. Take a minute to think like a scientist. Jot down in your nature journal how YOU think temperature is going to affect the glow. Put one of the glow sticks in the hot water and the other in the cold water. Wait a few minutes.

What is happening?

The glow stick in the hot water gets gradually brighter, while the glow stick in the cold water gets dimmer. Why do you think this is? The light energy is released faster in the hot water than in the cold. Fireflies light up more, and are more active when it is hotter outside, too.

MORE FUN: Which of the glow sticks do you think will lose its glow sooner? The one in the hot water or the one in the cold water? Why do you think this? Jot your hypothesis down in your journal and watch to see if you were right.

CATCHING FIREFLIES LIKE A BOSS!

ONE OF MY FAVORITE SUMMER EVENING ACTIVITIES IS CATCHING FIREFLIES AND OBSERVING THEM AS THEY CRAWL AROUND A JAR. YOU CAN DO THAT TOO—IT'S EASY!

GLASS JARS MAKE THE PERFECT BUG HABITAT FOR FIREFLIES. THIS IS A GREAT TIME TO USE UP ALL OF THOSE PICKLE, JELLY AND SPAGHETTI SAUCE JARS FROM THE RECYCLE BIN. JUST MAKE SURE YOU CLEAN THEM WELL—FIREFLIES DON'T MIX WELL WITH JELLY!

MATERIALS

Bug Net (page 17)

Glass jar (do NOT poke holes in its lid)

Grass clippings

A stick or leaves

A piece of an apple or potato

INSTRUCTIONS

Use your bug net to head outside and gently catch fireflies without hurting them.

When you have caught one, you can get it to crawl all by itself into the jar. Simply hold the jar upside down over top of it while it's in the net. Fireflies always crawl upwards.

Pretty cool trick, isn't it?

Put some grass clippings into the jar once your fireflies have crawled inside. Add a stick or some leaves for them to climb and a piece of potato or apple to the jar.

Make sure that you don't poke holes in the jar lids. Air holes dry the air inside of the jar out. Fireflies prefer damp air—which is why we see them outside on hot, humid nights. If you put a damp paper towel in the jar, and close the lid, there will be enough air for the fireflies you catch to stay alive for a day or two.

If you want to keep one or two of your fireflies for a few days to observe them, they'll be fine in your jar. Just open up the lid once or twice a day and blow across the top to displace and freshen the air. Fireflies don't eat. They did all their eating as larvae, so you don't need to worry about feeding them. But let them go after two or three days. Most fireflies only live a week or two, and they shouldn't have to spend all of their lives in a jar.

MORE FUN: **Every summer in Japan, people collect fireflies in jars and cages, then go out on boats together and let them go (often by the thousands) at the same time. The fireflies light up the sky at the firefly festivals in Japan. Invite your friends over for a firefly festival. Have them bring their own jars of fireflies and let them go together in your yard, and then play Hide and Glow Seek by hiding glow sticks all over the yard and trying to find them as the sky darkens.**

DARKLING BEETLE LIFECYCLES

WHILE DARKLING BEETLES ARE A LITTLE MORE CHALLENGING TO FIND
in your yard, they're so worth looking for. They're great decomposers, and they do amazing work breaking down rotting logs in woods and yards everywhere.

Their life cycle is easy to observe, and to experiment with. Darkling beetles are harmless to handle, and easy to care for. Take a look around outside—the scientific family name for darkling beetles, *Tenebrionidae*, means "one who loves darkness," so you'll find them in the dark places of your yard. Look under rocks, inside of rotting logs and branches, in the leaf litter under trees and other dark places like that.

You may find mealworms, the larval stage of the darkling beetle, more easily than the beetles themselves as they're larger and light-colored.

The beetles, though, can get to be up to an inch and a half (4 cm) long. They're covered with a brown or black armor-like shell. Most darkling beetles can complete their entire life cycle in 2 to 4 months, and they can be easily and safely handled in all of the stages they go through (except eggs). This makes them the perfect beetle to use when you want to observe an insect's entire life cycle.

LET'S GET STARTED!

FUN FACT: The darkling beetle can't fly. Their wings, called elytra, are fused and sealed to their abdomen. This makes them ideal insects to raise and observe at home, and might make your parents more likely to welcome them as temporary pets since they can't escape and fly around the house!

MAKE THE BEST HOME FOR YOUR BEETLES AND MEALWORMS!

DARKLING BEETLES AND THEIR LARVA ARE SUPER COOL TO RAISE. WE'VE RAISED THEM A FEW TIMES AT OUR HOUSE, AND ALL THE KIDS THAT COME OVER GET HOOKED ON MAKING MAZES AND OBSTACLE COURSES FOR THE MEALWORMS AND BEETLES. YOU CAN DO THAT TOO! IT'S SIMPLE AND FUN. CHECK IT OUT!

MATERIALS

Plastic or glass container with holes punched in the lid

Bedding (rolled oats, wheat bran, crushed cereal, ground corn or a mixture)

Chunk of a moist fruit or vegetable (potato, carrot, apple, etc.)

Mealworms and/or darkling beetles

INSTRUCTIONS

Setting up your habitat is super simple, and you'll likely have mealworms and beetles for months. It'll be like your own little beetle farm! Grab your materials and head outside.

Make sure that your container is clean and dry, and put in about a ½ inch (13 mm) of the bedding you chose. The bedding will be both a place for the beetles and larva to hide in, and food for them to eat.

Set a chunk of fruit or vegetable in there to provide moisture for the beetles and mealworms. Darkling beetles don't drink water. They get their moisture from the foods they eat. So they'll munch on the fruit to stay hydrated. You'll have to change it out for a new piece every day or two. It's important that you replace it before mold grows. You want to keep your beetles healthy.

Once it's set up, introduce your beetles and/or mealworms to their new home. They're pretty hardy insects, so you can just tip them into the habitat and they'll start eating.

If you had trouble finding mealworms or darkling beetles in your yard, you can get a little tub of mealworms from a local pet or birding store for $2.00 to $4.00. When my kids wanted to learn about mealworms, we ordered a big box of them on the Internet and had a blast! A population of mealworms is easy to maintain. We've kept them going for long periods of time to have a steady supply of live larva to feed our pet red eared sliders and the robins that love to visit our backyard every spring.

FUN FACT: Darkling beetles go through complete metamorphosis. This means that they go through all four stages—egg, larva, pupa and adult. Female beetles can lay up to 500 eggs at a time. The larva, or mealworms, hatch a few weeks later. Over the next two months, depending on the species, mealworms will molt 10 to 20 times before entering the pupal stage. About two weeks later, a whitish adult emerges. It turns brownish-black within 24 hours. They're pretty cool to observe—don't forget to draw their life cycles in your nature journal! You'll want to remember this!

COZY OATS, COMFY BRAN
MEALWORM EXPERIMENT ONE

WHAT DO YOU THINK MEALWORMS PREFER TO BE TUCKED IN WITH, OATS OR WHEAT BRAN? DO YOU THINK IT MATTERS TO THEM? USING A METHOD SIMILAR TO HOW YOU TESTED ROLY POLY ETHOLOGY (PAGE 28), YOU'LL SEE IF THEY CARE ONE WAY OR ANOTHER.

INSTEAD OF USING A CHOICE CONTAINER, THOUGH, YOU'LL JUST USE A FLAT TRAY. MEALWORMS ARE COOL TO EXPLORE, BUT THEY'RE NOT QUITE AS CURIOUS AS SOME OF THE OTHER INSECTS YOU'VE MAYBE EXPLORED. SEE WHAT I MEAN. . . .

MATERIALS

Large rectangular tray or container with high sides

Oats

Wheat bran

Mealworms

Your Nature Journal (page 12)

INSTRUCTIONS

Head outside and sit on the ground or at a picnic table. Spread a ½ inch (13 mm) of oats in the left third of the container and wheat bran in the right third of the container. Place 10 to 15 mealworms in the center of the container (the third with no bedding). Write your hypothesis in your nature journal. Which bedding do you think the majority of your mealworms will prefer? Why?

Leave your mealworms alone for about a half an hour. Read a book, play a quiet game or just listen to the sounds of nature—but stay close so you can make sure your mealworms are safe from predators like backyard birds. Check back to see if all of them have made their way over to one of the bedding options. Which type has the most mealworms? Sift through the oats and wheat bran and count the mealworms in each.

> MORE FUN: Try testing your mealworms' preference for other things—food, light, etc. You can do these same activities over again once they've metamorphosed to see if the beetles still behave in the same ways.

GETTING TO KNOW YOUR MEALWORMS AND BEETLES

THERE ARE SO MANY INTERESTING THINGS TO OBSERVE ABOUT MEALWORMS AND DARKLING BEETLES. AND SOMETIMES SCIENTISTS DO JUST THAT—OBSERVE. HERE'S YOUR CHANCE TO GET TO KNOW YOUR MEALWORMS AND BEETLES BETTER. WHO KNOWS WHAT YOU'LL DISCOVER!

MATERIALS

Your Nature Journal (page 12)

Mealworms and darkling beetles

A small tray or clear container

Magnifying glass, hand lens or pocket microscope

Mirror Box (page 18, optional)

INSTRUCTIONS

Grab your nature journal, something to write with and a few beetles and mealworms on a small tray or in a shallow container, and sit outside.

Using a magnifying glass, observe them carefully. Write and draw what you see happening in your journal. Here are some questions to get you started:

Can you tell the mealworms apart? How?

What is the distance a mealworm can travel in a minute? (Start it at one side of the tray, and mark where it stops after a minute. Then measure that distance and record it.)

What is the distance a darkling beetle can travel in a minute?

Can either the larvae or the beetles walk up a slanted surface? (Tip the tray or container to test this.)

Do the beetle's (or mealworm's) legs all move together when it walks? This is a good activity to observe using your Mirror Box from page 18.

What else do you observe about your mealworms' and beetles' behavior?

Often, scientists do activities like this again and again to see if the behaviors change over time. You can try this every few days to see if the beetles and mealworms act differently at different times of the day or during different seasons.

MORE FUN: Make a maze by gluing toothpicks to a piece of paper. Once the glue dries, put a piece of food or some shelter at the other end and time how long it takes your mealworm to find it. Test several times to see if its time got faster with each trial. We've also made fun mealworm mazes using wooden blocks on plastic trays so we can change them around again and again.

BIG BESS BEETLES

I HAVE TO ADMIT THAT BESS BEETLES (PASSALIDAE) MADE ME NERVOUS when I first started exploring and experimenting with backyard bugs and insects. They're pretty impressive with their pointy mandibles. Those front chompers are important, though, as bess beetles need them to eat and tunnel through decaying logs. So if you're not a piece of rotten wood, you're pretty safe when handling them.

Bess beetles are also called patent leather beetles because their shiny black exoskeleton looks like shiny patent leather shoes.

Have you seen these big beetles in logs of rotting trees in your yard or on nature walks? They can grow to be over an inch (2.5 cm) long!

Bess beetles have an important job. They're powerful decomposers and live in large family groups with two parents and many offspring working together to break down fallen trees and rotting logs. It's amazing, really.

You can find bess beetles all year long, holed up between the bark and the heart of the tree. And they're super cool to experiment with.

ARE YOU READY? LET'S GO!

GETTING TO KNOW YOUR BESS BEETLES

HEAD OUTSIDE WITH A CONTAINER AND PUT A SMALL LAYER OF DIRT AND A CHUNK OF ROTTING WOOD INSIDE. DIG THROUGH THE WOODPILE, LEAF LITTER, UNDER SHRUBS OR BUSHES OR ANYWHERE THAT STICKS, TWIGS OR LOGS MIGHT BE ROTTING. PULL APART THE BARK FROM THE WOOD AND LOOK FOR HOLES INSIDE THE LOGS. KEEP DIGGING UNTIL YOU FIND THE SHINY BLACK BEETLES CHEWING UP THAT WOOD. TRY TO GRAB TWO OR MORE IF YOU CAN. NOW, PUT TOGETHER THIS HABITAT AND WATCH THEM FOR A BIT. THEY'RE COOL TO OBSERVE!

MATERIALS

Clear container (plastic shoeboxes, pretzel containers or old plastic food storage containers work well)

Soil

Rotting wood (it should be decaying enough that you can easily break it apart with your hands)

Bess beetles

Spray bottle full of water

Magnifying glass, hand lens or pocket microscope

Your Nature Journal (page 12)

Mirror Box (page 18)

INSTRUCTIONS

Put your bess beetles in their new home. They are easy to care for, and can be kept for awhile, but it's always a good idea to release them back to the log where you found them when you're done observing them, as bess beetles need the stability of a large rotting log habitat in order to reproduce.

Since bess beetles look so intimidating with their large size and strong mandibles, this is a good time to get used to handling and observing them so that when you begin experimenting you'll have no trouble. They look scary, but they're not!

Bess beetles like humidity, so make sure to mist their habitat each day with your spray bottle. Don't get the wood too wet, though; you don't want it to get moldy.

Take your bess beetle out and let it walk on your hand. I promise that they're extremely gentle bugs. They won't bite you because, while their mandibles look like intimidating pinchers, they're made for chewing through wood. Are you daring enough to try it? Come on! You're brave . . . you can do it!

Let the beetle crawl around on your hand, and observe its movements using your magnifying glass. Draw a picture of it in your nature journal, then write about what it did while it was in your hands. Try putting it in your mirror box and see what it looks like from all angles.

What did it feel like? How quickly did it move? What did you notice about its mandibles when you looked at them through the magnifying glass? How can this help it eat through wood? Be a scientist and make detailed observations. They'll help you come to conclusions during your experiments on the next few pages.

FUN FACT: An adult bess beetle communicates by rubbing a hardened part of its hindwings against spines on the dorsal surface of its abdomen. This is called stridulation. Captive bess beetles will complain loudly when disturbed in any way. They'll also squeak when handled. Listen carefully. Can you hear them?

MIGHTY, MIGHTY BUGS
BESS BEETLE EXPERIMENT ONE

THIS IS AN EASY ACTIVITY TO DO WITH BESS BEETLES BECAUSE THEY'RE SO GENTLE AND EASY TO HANDLE. IT'S A GREAT DEMONSTRATION OF JUST HOW STRONG BEETLES REALLY ARE. YOU'LL TEST HOW MANY PENNIES A BEETLE CAN PULL—PREPARE TO BE AMAZED!

MATERIALS

Paper towel taped to a table outside

10- to 12-inch-long (25- to 30-cm) piece of waxed dental floss

Small plastic container

Pennies

Bess Beetles

Your Nature Journal (page 12)

INSTRUCTIONS

Head out to a table in the yard with your materials and your beetles. How many pennies do you think a bess beetle can pull? Take a minute and jot down your prediction in your nature journal.

Tie a loop on one end of your dental floss with a slip knot. You'll be looping this around the bess beetle's abdomen like a lasso, so you'll want it to be easy to resize.

Attach the other end to the plastic container.

Loop the lasso around your beetle's abdomen and tighten the loop gently. You want it tight enough so that it won't fall off, but not too tight. Remember that your bess beetles are living creatures, and it's important to handle them carefully while putting the lasso around their abdomen.

Don't put it on too tightly.

Place your beetle on one end of the paper towel. The towel will provide traction so it's easier for the beetle to walk. Put a penny in the container while the beetle pulls it.

Keep adding pennies carefully until the beetle stops moving, and isn't able to pull any more weight. Record the number of pennies the beetle was able to pull. Was your guess close?

Gently remove the harness from your beetle and put it back into its habitat. Let it rest for a while before you take it out to play again.

FUN FACT: Most insects lay their eggs and leave them. Bess beetles are different. Both the mother and the father stick around to raise babies. In fact, older larvae help with their little siblings, too. Does your family help each other out like bess beetle families do?

INCREDIBLE BEETLE CHARIOT RACES

DO YOU WANT TO HAVE MORE FUN WITH THE PULLING POWER OF BESS BEETLES? LET YOUR FRIENDS REST UP FOR A FEW DAYS AFTER YOU TEST HOW MUCH WEIGHT THEY CAN PULL, AND THEN RIG UP TWO FRESH LASSOS WITH SLIP KNOTS AND ATTACH THEM TO YOUR BEETLES CAREFULLY.

SEE HOW QUICKLY THEY CAN CARRY YOUR LITTLE PEOPLE TO THE FINISH LINE.

MATERIALS

Paper towel, taped to a table

2 Bess Beetle Lassos (page 61)

2 small plastic containers

2 small toy people

Bess beetles

INSTRUCTIONS

Go outside and draw a start line and a finish line on a paper towel, and hook the beetles' lassos to two same-sized plastic containers. Tape the paper towel to a table top. Place a small plastic person in each container. Try to find same-sized, light-weight people so the race is fair.

Place your two chariot-driving bess beetles at the start line and loop the lassos around their abdomens. This is a fun activity to do with a friend. Release them and see which pulls their chariot to the finish line first. Cheer your racer on!

FUN FACT: There are a lot of nicknames for the bess beetle. They're a member of the *Passalidae* family and can be called bessbugs, bessie bugs, betsy beetles, horned passalus beetle, patent leather beetles, peg beetles and horn beetles. Many of those nicknames stem from the French word *baiser* which means "to kiss." It refers to their stridulation, which sounds like they're smooching.

BOUNDING, BOUNCING CRICKETS

I'LL NEVER FORGET THE DAY my husband and I were hiking through a meadow with our oldest kiddo (and our only one at the time). It was hot, sticky and very buggy. My son took a step and the biggest grasshopper I'd ever seen in my life jumped up at him, hit him in the head and hopped away.

He screamed and went running out of the meadow yelling, "Help! I'm being chased by a wild *aminal*!" It was funny. Not only because he'd mispronounced animal, but also because it was an insect. Harmless and common.

Have you ever been there? Afraid of something so harmless? Crickets and grasshoppers move quickly and can be startling, but they're not scary. In fact, they're pretty cool once you start to learn about them.

Crickets (*Gryllidae*) are often easier to get and capture, so we're going to focus on those in this section. Did you know that male crickets chirp to attract a female mate? Male crickets make their chirping noise by rubbing their wings together. Since they are usually nocturnal we hear them at dusk and at night.

Before you get started with the activities in this chapter, you'll need to find some crickets to gather. Crickets can be found in grassy and sandy areas around the country, so go hunting in your yard late in the day or early in the evening. Crickets are harmless, so just scoop them in your cupped hands or in the bug net from page 17. If you're really having trouble finding them, though, you can get them at the pet store for about a dollar a dozen. If you happen to catch a grasshopper instead of a cricket, you can use it instead.

FUN FACT: Crickets are a huge source of protein in many countries including Cambodia—they're eaten roasted, fried, raw and even ground up in flour! Hmmm . . . are you hungry for cricket cookies?

BRIGHT AND BREEZY DIGS FOR YOUR CRICKETS

CRICKETS ARE EASY TO KEEP, AND WILL CHIRP IN THE EARLY EVENING, GIVING YOU PLENTY OF LULLABIES TO LULL YOU TO SLEEP. REAL WHITE NOISE FOR YOUR ROOM! LEARN HOW TO MAKE THE BEST HOME FOR THEM—THEY'LL LOVE THEIR NEW 'DIGS."

MATERIALS

Plastic or glass container with a vented lid (you can use one of your bug boxes from page 15)

Sand

Branches, egg cartons, cardboard tubes, etc.

Piece of fruit or vegetable

Small square of sponge

Your Nature Journal (page 12)

INSTRUCTIONS

Head outside with your materials, and find a comfortable place to make this project. You can start making your cricket friends comfy right away by spreading a layer of sand on the bottom of your container.

Put some twigs, pieces of cardboard tubes or egg cartons, or other things on the bottom so they have somewhere to hide. Crickets love to hide!

Crickets will eat almost anything. You can feed them bits of fruit and vegetables, but you'll need to keep an eye on it to make sure it doesn't spoil. Replace the food with fresh pieces as it dries out or gets old.

Your crickets can easily drown in standing water, so place a piece of damp sponge in the container so they can drink from it. You'll love watching these little critters!

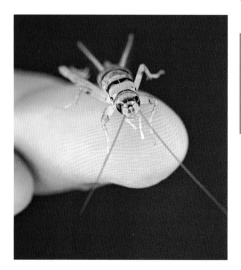

FUN FACT: Crickets have been kept as pets in China for centuries. They're considered good luck, and you can still find street vendors there selling pet crickets in little bamboo cages today. See . . . doing the activities in this book can actually bring you good luck!

FIRST-RATE CRICKET THERMOMETERS

ON A DAY WHEN THE TEMPERATURE FALLS BETWEEN 55 AND 100 DEGREES FAHRENHEIT (13 TO 38°C), HEAD OUTSIDE TO WHERE YOU NORMALLY HEAR CRICKETS OR BRING THE PETS YOU'VE ALREADY CAPTURED TO A SHADY AREA IN THE YARD.

LET THEM RELAX AND START CHIRPING. PRETTY SOON, THEY'LL START TO TELL YOU WHAT THE TEMPERATURE IS OUT THERE.

MATERIALS

Crickets (or a spot in your yard where you usually see or hear them)

Stopwatch

Outdoor thermometer

Your Nature Journal (page 12)

INSTRUCTIONS

Pick out the sound of one cricket and use your stopwatch to count the number of chirps you hear in 14 seconds. Add that number to 40. The answer you get should be close to the temperature in degrees Fahrenheit. (To determine temperature in Celsius, count the chirps in 25 seconds, divide that count by 3, then add 4.)

It's as simple as that. Really!

You can get even more accurate if you do this several times and take the average result. Do you know how to figure out averages? Say you calculated the temperature five times, and you got 70, 71, 71, 74 and 72. You would add those results together to get 358. Then, you divide that number (358) by the number of temperatures you had added together (5). Your average temperature would be 71.6 degrees Fahrenheit.

Check the outdoor thermometer. I bet you were pretty close. Crickets are amazing at telling us the temperature of the air around us.

Pretty cool, huh?

FUN FACT: Female crickets can lay up to 200 eggs at a time. Imagine how many little cricket thermometers you could have in your yard!

WET SAND, DRY SAND
CRICKET EXPERIMENT ONE

YOU'VE MADE YOUR CRICKETS A HOME, BUT DID YOU THINK ABOUT THE CONDITIONS IN WHICH YOU FOUND THEM? DO YOU THINK THEY'D PREFER WET OR DAMP SAND TO THE DRY SAND YOU PUT IN THERE? LET'S CHECK IT OUT AND SEE WHAT THEY LIKE!

MATERIALS

Small lidded container

Sand

Water

Your Nature Journal (page 12)

Crickets

INSTRUCTIONS

Grab your clean container and head outside, and then spread dry sand on one side of the container. Get some sand wet (but not too wet—you don't want standing water) and put it on the other side. You can't use your Choice Container (page 26) for this because the crickets would likely just hide in the center tube. They like to cozy up in small spaces.

Make a hypothesis. Write down which side you think the majority of the crickets will go to in your nature journal. Write down your reasons for thinking that, too.

Place your crickets in the center of the sand choices, and leave them alone for 10 to 15 minutes. Check back. Where are most of your crickets now? Are they on the wet or dry side? Why do you think that is? Write down your results and why you think that happened.

Depending on how damp it is, the crickets might have liked that side better. While they don't like wet ground, they do like it cool and moist. So, the next time you walk by their habitat, you might want to mist it with a spray bottle.

MORE FUN: **Try testing other cricket preferences, too. What other experiments can you come up with? Maybe you can test different food choices, or whether they have color preferences or the light versus the dark. The possibilities are endless.**

TOGETHER BUGS, LONELY BUGS
CRICKET EXPERIMENT TWO

DO YOU THINK THAT CRICKETS PREFER TO LIVE ALONE OR WITH OTHERS LIKE THEM? WHY DO YOU THINK THAT? WRITE DOWN YOUR HYPOTHESIS IN YOUR NATURE JOURNAL. THEN, GET READY TO TEST IT OUT AND SEE WHAT YOUR CRICKETS DO.

MATERIALS

1 cardboard tube per cricket

Container with a thin layer of sand on the bottom

2 or more crickets

Your Nature Journal (page 12)

INSTRUCTIONS

Put the cardboard tubes inside the container, bring it all outside, then set your crickets gently on the sand. Check back every 5 to 10 minutes to see what your crickets are doing. Are they together? Apart? Chirping?

Finally, after 40 minutes, write down your results in your nature journal. Draw your container and where the crickets all ended up. Most of the crickets should have decided to find their own hiding spot. They're solitary insects that prefer to live alone.

If you heard chirping, though, you had at least one male in the container, and he may have been interested in attracting one of the females.

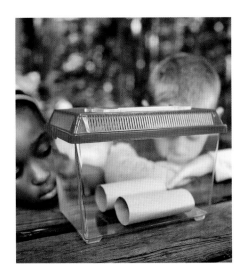

FUNNIES: WHAT'S AN INSECT'S FAVORITE SPORT?
CRICKET!

CHECKING OUT EARTHWORMS

A few years ago, I couldn't get my girls to touch worms—no matter what I told them. It didn't matter that they were harmless. It didn't matter that they felt cool and rubbery. It didn't matter that they were everywhere in our garden. My daughters wouldn't have anything to do with earthworms.

Until they found one drying out on the driveway one sunny morning. . . .

Earthworms breathe through their skin, and need their skin to stay moist, so my girls were upset about this poor worm dying on the driveway. And they wanted to help, but they still didn't want to touch it. Between the two of them, they made a little cloth stretcher and soaked it in water, then carefully lifted the worm onto the stretcher with a stick.

IT WAS AN INTERESTING SIGHT.

They spent that summer learning everything they could about earthworms. There are over 6,000 species of earthworm in the world. The most common ones found in your yard are the night crawler (it comes out at night), the angleworm (a good bait worm) and the rain worm (which comes out of waterlogged soil after it rains).

Worm eggs look like itty bitty lemons. Baby worms are teeny, tiny, fully-formed worms right as they emerge from the egg. They reach maturity in about a year, but can live up to ten years! Most species can grow to be about 14 inches (36 cm) long, but Australia's Giant Gippsland earthworm can grow to be over 9 feet (3 m) long!

Can you imagine a worm that long in your garden? Whoa!

A worm's digestive system is a tube that runs straight from its mouth all the way through to the end of its body. Most species eat fallen leaves and plant material. This makes worms important movers of nutrients like potassium and nitrogen.

Now that my girls have learned so much about worms, they often have several they're keeping to study as pets. They keep them in little miniature worm bins, and let them go after a few days. It's your turn to try out some of the activities and experiments my kids have loved trying with their worms.

They love holding them now. Have you held a worm before? So many people think they'll be slimy, but they really feel more rubbery than anything. Cool, damp and rubbery. . . . They're fun to play with.

And . . . you can have some fun with your friends who don't like worms, too. My six-year-old chased around a buddy of hers holding out one of her worm friends to scare him—but I promise that no worms were harmed in the episode, and he's now a worm lover, too!

THE MOST COLOSSAL WORM HOME YOU CAN MAKE

IF YOU WANT TO KEEP YOUR WORMS AT HOME FOR A WHILE, THIS IS ONE OF OUR FAVORITE HOMEMADE WORM HABITATS. YOUR WORMY FRIENDS CAN LIVE IN IT FOR A LONG, LONG TIME IF YOU TAKE GOOD CARE OF THEM. LET'S GO BUILD, CONSTRUCTION WORKERS!

MATERIALS

Clean 2-liter bottle

Craft knife

Small rocks or gravel

Unfertilized potting or garden soil

Cornmeal

Dry, dead leaves

Chopped fruits and vegetables

Spray bottle with water

Worms

Plastic wrap

Rubber bands

Your Nature Journal (page 12)

INSTRUCTIONS

Do this activity in the driveway or yard so you can brush away any spilled dirt when you're done. Take the label off your 2-liter bottle, and have an adult help you cut the top off with the craft knife.

Spread an inch (2.5 cm) of gravel on the bottom of the bottle, and place several inches (8 to 12 cm) of soil on top of the gravel.

For the top layer, mix cornmeal, leaves and food scraps together. This is the food layer for your worms. They'll eat this and break it down into compost. Lightly spritz this top layer with your spray bottle, being careful not to soak it.

Gently place a few worms in the habitat (two to four work well), and stretch plastic wrap over the top. Secure the plastic wrap with a rubber band and poke a few holes into it for ventilation.

Now you have a safe home for your worms, and a mini vermicomposting bin, too! Vermicomposting is a method of composting that uses worms to do what they do best—break down plant matter into super healthy soil. Every few days, add a little bit of food to the habitat and spray it lightly with your spray bottle.

MORE FUN: If you want to encourage your worms to hang out near the sides of the habitat where you can see them, then cover the outside of the bottle with dark-colored paper or cloth and put it in a cool, dark place for a few days. When you uncover it, you should see the layers and any tunnels the worms have made. You can hold tracing paper up to your habitat and trace their tunnels, then tape that into your nature journal.

WET WORMS, DRY WORMS
EARTHWORM EXPERIMENT ONE

YOU FIND WORMS OUT ON THE DRIVEWAY AND SIDEWALK AFTER A HEAVY RAIN WHERE THEY GO TO ESCAPE THE FLOODED SOIL. DOES THAT MEAN THAT THEY DON'T LIKE MOISTURE, THOUGH? IT'S INTERESTING, ISN'T IT? THERE ARE SO MANY THINGS IN NATURE THAT SEEM CONTRADICTORY. THIS MIGHT BE ONE OF THOSE THINGS.

TRY IT OUT, THOUGH. FIND OUT JUST WHICH CONDITIONS YOUR WORMS REALLY DO PREFER. . . . HERE WE GO!

MATERIALS

Your Nature Journal (page 12)

Two paper towels—one damp, one dry

Shallow container or tray

Three or four worms

INSTRUCTIONS

What do you think? Do earthworms prefer their habitats to be wet or dry? Think about where you found your worms, and write your hypothesis in your nature journal.

Put your wet paper towel flat on one side or your container, and set your container on a table outside in the yard. Place the dry towel on the other side, making sure that they overlap a bit in the center.

Put your worms right in the middle where the paper towels meet, and leave your worms alone for about 30 minutes.

When you come back, observe where your worms are. Did they all crawl to the same side? Which did they choose? Why do you think that is?

Worms tend to like moist soil, so they probably all crawled to the damp paper towel.

> **MORE FUN:** Make worm-y ice pops by putting sour gummy worms into ice pop molds, then pouring your favorite fruit drink over top of them. Freeze until they are solid and enjoy! Now you can tell friends you like to eat worms for a snack!

LIGHT WORMS, DARK WORMS
EARTHWORM EXPERIMENT TWO

THINK ABOUT WHAT YOU KNOW ABOUT EARTHWORMS SO FAR. DO EARTHWORMS PREFER THEIR HABITATS TO BE LIGHT OR DARK? THINK ABOUT WHERE YOU FOUND YOUR WORMS, AND WRITE YOUR HYPOTHESIS IN YOUR NATURE JOURNAL. ONCE YOU'RE DONE WRITING OUT YOUR HYPOTHESIS, LET'S WORK TOGETHER TO FIND OUT THE ANSWER!

MATERIALS

Shallow container or tray

A dark cloth

Three or four worms

Your Nature Journal (page 12)

INSTRUCTIONS

Set your container on a sturdy table or on the driveway. Put your worms in the center of the container and wrap one half of it in a dark cloth. Leave the other half exposed to light.

Let your worms hang out for about 30 minutes.

When you come back, observe where your worms are. Did they all crawl to the same side? Which did they choose? Why do you think that is?

Worms tend to like dark soil, so they probably all crawled to the dark side of the container. Think about where you find worms—under rocks and in the soil. It just makes sense, doesn't it?

FUNNIES: WHAT IS IT CALLED WHEN WORMS TAKE OVER THE WORLD?
GLOBAL WORMING!

BRIGHT LIGHTS, SENSITIVE WORMS
EARTHWORM EXPERIMENT THREE

YOU DISCOVERED THAT WORMS PREFER DARK HABITATS IN THE PREVIOUS ACTIVITY, BUT HOW SENSITIVE ARE THEY TO THE LIGHT? AND, ARE CERTAIN PARTS OF THEIR BODIES MORE SENSITIVE THAN OTHERS? LET'S SEE!

MATERIALS

Your Nature Journal (page 12)

Piece of cardboard that will fit over the flashlight

Flashlight

Tape

Shallow container or tray

Lid or cloth to cover half of the container or tray

Worms

INSTRUCTIONS

You can make some predictions about what will happen in your journal. Which part of an earthworm's body will be the most sensitive to the light? Why do you think that? Write your answers down, then head outside to experiment.

Poke a hole in the center of the cardboard. You'll be taping this to the light on the flashlight to make a concentrated point of light. You don't want the light to be too big, but you want it to be big enough to light up a part of the worm.

Tape your cardboard over the light on the flashlight and test it by turning it on and pointing it towards the tray. Does a small point of light shine? Perfect. Put the lid or cloth over one half of the tray to create a shaded area for your worm to retreat to if it gets stressed.

Now, put a worm gently on the tray and shine your light at one of its ends. What happens? Shine your light at its middle. Does it react the same way? How is it reacting differently? What about its other end? Is that sensitive to the light? What happens when you shine your light there?

When my kids did this activity, they found that their worms were more sensitive to the light when they shined it on their ends. Was your experience the same as theirs? Remember, too, that worms are living creatures and you don't want to hurt them. If one gets too stressed by the light, let it hang out in the shaded area of your tray and grab another worm to test further. Respect your worm friends!

MORE FUN: Worms are sensitive to, and dislike, light. But, what about colored light? Do you think they'll react the same way if you expose them to colored points of light? You can easily make your flashlight shine colored light on your worms by gathering three colored Magnatiles toys, food container lids or another transparent colored thing you find around your house. Just put the color on the flashlight and tape it to it with the hole-punched cardboard. Do the same thing you did in the light experiment. Point the colored light to the worms' ends and middle sections. Do they react differently when different colored lights are shined on them?

STRONG SMELLS, WEAK SMELLS
EARTHWORM EXPERIMENT FOUR

IF WORMS DON'T HAVE NOSES, DO THEY HAVE A SENSE OF SMELL? WILL THEY REACT TO DIFFERENT ODORS WHEN SURROUNDED BY DIFFERENT CHOICES? FIND OUT HOW SENSITIVE THEY ARE TO SMELLS IN THIS SIMPLE EXPERIMENT.

MATERIALS

Paper towel

Sharpie

Water

Cotton balls

Three different items with a strong scent

Your Nature Journal (page 12)

Worms

MORE FUN: Try to design your own experiment. Can you figure out a way to do this experiment to see where the most chemoreceptors are on a worm's body? And, do you think it matters what type of worm you test (earthworm, night crawler, red wiggler, etc.)? What about the size/age of the worm? Do you think that matters?

There are so many ways you can extend your scientific study of worm chemoreceptors. If you design a new experiment, let me know about it. Ask your parents if you can email me a picture or description of your new experiment (see page 203). I can't wait to see what you come up with!

INSTRUCTIONS

Set your paper towel on a table outside. Use your sharpie to divide it into four quadrants. Label each section with one of the three different scents you'll be using. We used an orange slice, dish soap and mint oil. Label the fourth quadrant with the word Control. That will be your control for the experiment.

A control is something that represents the normal state of something. In this case, you'll be trying to answer the question, "Can worms smell?" By having a section with nothing in it, you're able to have a section with little to no smell.

Once you label your paper towel, get the whole thing damp and spread it out on a table or tray. Rub your three scents all over the cotton balls (one on each) and place them in whichever quadrant is labeled with their name. For example, we placed our orange juice soaked cotton ball in the section labeled Orange. Leave the Control section alone.

Draw your testing area in your nature journal so you have a record of what is happening. Do you think worms can smell? Will they stay away from certain scents? Will they be drawn to certain scents?

Gently place a worm down in the center of the paper towel. Observe its movements. What is happening? Is it just sitting there? Is it moving around? Draw and write what you're observing in your nature journal. Let the worm hang out on the paper towel for at least 10 minutes. Did it stop moving?

Put it back in the habitat and test a different worm. What did this worm do? Did it react in the same way as the other worm? You can try this with many different worms and write down your observations.

So, what is the answer? Could you tell definitively if the worms you placed on the paper towel could smell the scents? Maybe . . . maybe not. Some kids who have tried this experiment see their worms react strongly to specific scents. Others don't.

The truth is that worms don't actually smell and taste things the way we do. They have special chemoreceptors that are found in their skin. They sense both smell and taste through those chemoreceptors. While there are chemoreceptors all over their bodies, worms have a more concentrated amount of them near their heads and tails. So . . . they kind of have noses all over their bodies!

HEART TO HEART TO HEART: EARTHWORM HEARTS

IMAGINE IF YOU HAD FIVE SEPARATE HEARTS BEATING TOGETHER IN YOUR BODY. HOW QUICKLY COULD YOUR BLOOD TRAVEL THEN? EARTHWORMS HAVE FIVE HEARTS LOCATED IN THEIR ANTERIOR SECTION. TOGETHER, THESE FIVE HEARTS MOVE BLOOD TO ALL AREAS OF THE WORM'S BODY. MOST EARTHWORMS GROW TO BE ABOUT 12 INCHES (30 CM) LONG.

HUMANS BREATHE USING LUNGS. OXYGEN AND CARBON DIOXIDE ARE EXCHANGED WITH EACH BREATH. ALTHOUGH EARTHWORMS HAVE MANY HEARTS, THEY DO NOT HAVE LUNGS. THEY BREATHE THROUGH THEIR SKIN. THEIR BODIES MUST STAY MOIST FOR THEM TO BE ABLE TO BREATHE.

IN THIS ACTIVITY, YOU CAN SEE A WORM'S HEARTS AT WORK. WATCH CAREFULLY—THEY BEAT QUICKLY!

MATERIALS

Your Nature Journal (page 12)

Paper towels

Spray bottle filled with water

Petri or other clear dish

Worm

Magnifying glass (or a microscope if you have one)

Watch or clock with second hand OR a timer

INSTRUCTIONS

Take your pulse by placing two fingers (not your thumb!) at your wrist and counting the beats for one minute. Record your pulse in your nature journal.

Place your earthworm on a moist paper towel or in a clear dish that has been spritzed with water.

To observe your earthworm's heartbeats, find the clitellum, or saddle area, that's the thick band on the worm's body. The anterior section is the shorter end of the body. Your worm's mouth is at the very tip of the anterior section of the worm. An earthworm's hearts lie very close together about halfway between the mouth tip and the saddle.

For a clearer view of the heartbeats, look closely through a magnifying glass and locate the hearts. My kids like to hold their worms above them in a container when they're outside so the sun shines down on it.

Notice that the hearts seem to ripple as they beat. Each ripple is made up of the five hearts beating one after another, one time. This ripple counts as one heartbeat. Make sure to spritz your worm with water if it gets dry.

Set a timer for one minute so you can count your worm's heartbeat. This is your worm's pulse. Figure out how many times the earthworm's hearts beat for every one of your heartbeats by dividing the worm's pulse by your pulse.

(continued)

HEART TO HEART TO HEART: EARTHWORM HEARTS (CONT.)

Here's a challenge for you—do some math to figure out whether your heart, or the worm's hearts will beat more over the course of a lifetime. On average, healthy humans live for approximately 78 years. Multiply the following:

YOUR PULSE (HEARTBEATS PER MINUTE) × 60 MINUTES = YOUR HEARTBEATS PER HOUR

YOUR HEARTBEATS PER HOUR × 24 HOURS = YOUR HEARTBEATS PER DAY

YOUR HEARTBEATS PER DAY × 365 = YOUR HEARTBEATS PER YEAR

YOUR HEARTBEATS PER YEAR × 78 = YOUR HEARTBEATS PER LIFETIME

An earthworm can live for about ten years if it avoids becoming another animal's prey. Try this formula to determine how many times an earthworm's heart will beat over its lifetime:

EARTHWORM'S PULSE (HEARTBEATS PER MINUTE) × 60 MINUTES = EARTHWORM'S HEARTBEATS PER HOUR

EARTHWORM'S HEARTBEATS PER HOUR × 24 HOURS = EARTHWORM'S HEARTBEATS PER DAY

EARTHWORM'S HEARTBEATS PER DAY × 365 = EARTHWORM'S HEARTBEATS PER YEAR

EARTHWORM'S HEARTBEATS PER YEAR × 10 = EARTHWORM'S HEARTBEATS PER LIFETIME

Which one—you or the earthworm—will have more heartbeats over the course of a lifetime?

FUN FACT: The longest earthworm ever discovered was found in South Africa. It was almost 264 inches (6.7 m) long! That worm's hearts had to push its blood a long way!

PUTTING WORMS TO WORK

YOU MADE A LITTLE WORM HABITAT ALREADY WITH THE ACTIVITY ON PAGE 74, BUT DID YOU KNOW THAT WORMS ARE FABULOUS WORKERS THAT CAN REALLY HELP YOUR GARDEN GROW? IT'S TRUE. VERMICOMPOSTING IS A GREAT WAY TO GET NUTRIENT-RICH GARDEN SOIL FOR YOUR PLANTS.

AND YOUR WORMS WILL HAPPILY WORK FOR YOU ALL YEAR ROUND, WITH VERY LITTLE MAINTENANCE AND A BIT OF FOOD SCRAPS. YOU CAN MAKE YOUR OWN VERMICOMPOSTING BIN IN THIS ACTIVITY!

MATERIALS

Two 8 to 10 gallon (30 to 37 L) plastic storage containers

Drill with ¼-inch (6-mm) and ¹⁄₁₆-inch (1-mm) bits

Shredded newspaper

Unfertilized soil or dirt and leaf litter

About a pound (450 g) of worms (you can hunt for them, or order some online to kick-start the project)

Piece of cardboard

INSTRUCTIONS

Have an adult help you with this project. Drill about 20 to 30 ¼-inch (6-mm) holes in the bottom of the containers. This will allow for drainage and for the worms to wriggle through when you're ready to harvest your worm castings. Worm castings are the waste left by a worm after it breaks down organic waste. They're full of nutrients that plants love.

Drill ¹⁄₁₆-inch (1-mm) ventilation holes around the top of each container about an inch (2.5 cm) apart, and about 20 to 30 on the lid. This will allow air to flow well around the top of the bin.

Remember that worms like their habitats moist, but not wet. Shred the newspaper and soak it in water. Then, wring the paper out completely so that it's just damp. Add it to one of the worm bins, and fluff it up. Put a thin layer of dirt and leaf litter on top of the newspaper. Put the worms in the bin and let them get acclimated for a few days before you add any other food.

Put the cardboard on top of the newspaper and leaf litter. Put the second, empty, bin on the cardboard and cover that with the ventilated lid.

Place the worms into the bin and find a nice shady place outside to store the bin. Put the bin on top of blocks or bricks to allow for drainage. Use the lid of the second bin as a tray to catch any moisture that may drain from the bin. This worm tea is a great liquid fertilizer.

If it gets too hot or too cold, bring the worm bin inside and put it in the basement or in the laundry room. Otherwise, they'll live and work happily outside for you.

(continued)

Feed your worms slowly at first. As the worms multiply, you can begin to add more food. Gently bury food scraps (fruits, vegetable, grains, cleaned eggshells or coffee grounds—no meat, eggs or cheese) in a different section of the bin each week, under the cardboard. The worms will follow the food scraps around the bin.

About a month or two before you're ready to harvest the castings to use in your garden, add newspaper, dirt, leaf litter and a bit of food to the top bin. Stop adding food to the bottom bin. The worms will migrate up through the drainage holes to get to the food in the top bin, and then you can dump the contents of the bottom bin into your garden.

Then, place the now empty bin on top, and let the process begin again. A healthy worm bin will continue to work for you for years.

MORE FUN: Want to gather lots of worms at once? Take a large piece of cardboard and get it damp. Leave it out in your grass overnight and check it early the next morning. You should find dozens of worms, ready to be added to your vermicompost bin!

CATERPILLARS AND BUTTERFLIES

FINDING AND RAISING CATERPILLARS IS SUCH A COOL THING TO DO!

Caterpillars can be found all over. Some grow to be moths and others become butterflies. Butterflies and moths are part of the order *Lepidoptera*. Regardless of the type you find, you need to be very observant if you hope to raise them successfully.

Caterpillars are very, very picky. They usually can only survive on one or two types of plants, usually the plant on which you find them. For example, monarch butterflies can only survive by eating leaves of the milkweed plant.

AND CATERPILLARS EAT A LOT.

AND POOP A LOT.

Really! If you want to raise caterpillars well, then make sure you have lots of their preferred food to feed them and clean their jar or tank often.

You can encourage butterflies to lay eggs in your yard by building butterfly feeders and planting host plants for their caterpillars. Remember, though, that butterflies need fuel too, so plant both caterpillar host plants and nectar flowers for the butterflies.

Butterflies like flowers such as coneflower, butterfly bush, black-eyed susans, sedums, hollyhocks, aster and marigold. Caterpillars like milkweed (monarchs), spicebush (spicebush swallowtail), paw-paw (zebra swallowtail), parsley, dill, fennel (black swallowtail), walnut and sweet gum (luna moth), and cherry (cecropia moth and viceroy).

You can also attract butterflies with some of the easy feeders in this chapter. Ready to set up the most epic backyard butterfly habitat in the neighborhood? Awesome! Let's go!

SUPER SIMPLE YOGURT LID FEEDER

THIS IS PROBABLY ONE OF THE EASIEST BUTTERFLY FEEDERS YOU'LL EVER MAKE. ALL YOU NEED IS A FEW SIMPLE SUPPLIES FROM AROUND THE HOUSE AND YOU'RE GOOD TO GO! LET'S DO IT!

MATERIALS

Lid from a plastic yogurt container

Hole punch

Yarn, cut into 3 to 4 long pieces

Pony beads

Very ripe fruit

Your Nature Journal (page 12)

INSTRUCTIONS

Punch three or four holes around the edge of the lid. You want them to be equidistant from one another because you'll use these to tie on the yarn and hang your feeder.

Tie the yarn to the holes, and thread pony beads on the yarn to decorate your feeder. Once you have your beads all strung, tie the three or four pieces of yarn together at the top, and hang it near your flowers. Put the ripe fruit on the lid once it's hung securely.

And there you go! I told you it was easy! Now you can observe beautiful butterflies enjoying the fruit in your feeder and make cool scientific notes about them in your nature journal.

FUNNIES: WHAT DO INSECTS STUDY AT SCHOOL?

MOTHEMATICS!

GROOVY GARDEN BUTTERFLY FEEDING CENTER

LOOKING FOR SOMETHING TO GIVE YOUR BUTTERFLY VISITORS MORE OF A REASON TO STAY IN THE YARD? THIS FEEDING STATION IS JUST THE TICKET! IT TAKES A LITTLE MORE ENERGY TO PUT TOGETHER THAN THE SUPER SIMPLE YOGURT LID BUTTERFLY FEEDER ON PAGE 90, BUT IT'S SO WORTH THE EXTRA EFFORT! YOUR GARDEN IS GOING TO LOOK SO SUPER GROOVY!

MATERIALS

2 (14-inch [35-cm]) terra cotta pots

Epoxy (optional)

1 (20-inch [50-cm]) terra cotta saucer

River rocks or gravel

Small potted flower or herb varieties that butterflies love (we used dill and parsley)

Water

Fruit

Your Nature Journal (page 12)

INSTRUCTIONS

Turn one of the pots upside down in the center of your butterfly garden. Place the other pot right-side up on top of it. (You could glue the two pots together with epoxy if you want your structure to be permanent—just make sure you get your parent's help because it is a permanent adhesive. We decided not to because we wanted to be able to stack it easily to store it for the winter.)

Put the saucer on top of the top pot and fill with about an inch (2.5 cm) of water. Make little islands with the river stones or gravel so that butterflies have a place to perch as they drink. Also in the water, put the herb or flowerpots on one side, and the fruit on the other. We like to put out orange slices and sideways slices of banana.

Clean out the fruit regularly, replacing with fresh, and clean and freshen the water, too, so that visitors always have fresh water to drink. Make sure you head outside regularly to observe the visitors you get. Try drawing them in your nature journal so you keep a record of the types of butterflies that stop by for visits.

FUN FACT: Did you know that butterflies don't build a chrysalis; they shed their final layer of skin to reveal the chrysalis underneath. I wonder . . . do you think a caterpillar will form its chrysalis in your butterfly garden? How cool will that be?

SPECTACULAR SPONGE FEEDER FOR BUTTERFLIES

THIS IS PROBABLY ONE OF THE EASIEST BUTTERFLY FEEDERS EVER! FOR REAL! BUT, JUST BECAUSE IT'S EASY TO MAKE, DON'T THINK IT'S LESS APPEALING FOR YOUR BUTTERFLY FRIENDS! THEY'LL LOVE IT JUST AS MUCH AS THE OTHERS IN THIS CHAPTER!

MATERIALS

Sponge (without a scrubber side)

Hole punch

Garden twine

Sensationally Sweet Butterfly Nectar (recipe below)

Your Nature Journal (page 12)

INSTRUCTIONS

Grab the things you need and head outside to make this easy-peasy butterfly treat! Simply punch a hole in the top of the sponge and thread garden twine through it. Tie it tightly and hang it near flowers or bushes.

Dip it into a jar of butterfly nectar every day or two days, depending on the heat and how quickly it dries out. Use your nature journal to track the butterflies that visit and how often they come.

> FUN FACT: Butterflies taste with their feet. Can you imagine that? What if you had to taste with YOUR feet? Yuck!

SENSATIONALLY SWEET BUTTERFLY NECTAR

THOSE GORGEOUS GARDEN VISITORS NEED SOMETHING TO FUEL THEM UP AS THEY DO THE TOUGH WORK OF FINDING SOMEWHERE TO LAY THEIR EGGS. SWEETEN THEIR VISIT WITH THIS YUMMY BUTTERFLY TREAT.

MATERIALS

½ cup (96 g) sugar

2 cups (473 ml) water

Saucepan

Glass jar with a lid

Spectacular Sponge Feeder for Butterflies (above)

INSTRUCTIONS

Have an adult help you use the stove. Mix the sugar and water together in the saucepan and bring to a boil. Stir it until all the sugar is dissolved. Pour the nectar into the glass jar and let it cool.

Dip the nectar feeder into the jar, or squirt some nectar on it with a medicine syringe or pipette. Refrigerate the rest of the nectar until you need it.

SLEUTHING & CARING FOR CATERPILLARS

BUTTERFLIES AND MOTHS ARE EASY TO KEEP AND OBSERVE AT HOME. THEY'RE PRETTY AWESOME TO WATCH AS THEY EAT AND EAT THEIR WAY THROUGH DIFFERENT LIFE STAGES. WE'VE KEPT A JAR OF CATERPILLARS ON OUR KITCHEN TABLE EVERY SPRING SINCE OUR OLDEST CHILD WAS TWO YEARS OLD. YOU CAN TOO!

MATERIALS

Glass aquarium, plastic container or gallon (3.8-L) jar

Stick that can fit diagonally in your container

Host plants (for caterpillars to eat)

Spray bottle

FUN FACT: Birdwing butterflies have angular wings and fly just like birds do. I love that different species of animals often mimic each other. Nature is so cool!

INSTRUCTIONS

Butterflies and moths start their lives as eggs. When they hatch, they eat their egg shell first, then immediately need to start munching on their host plant. That's why female butterflies and moths lay their eggs on the leaves of caterpillar host plants, usually. It ensures that their caterpillars will be well taken care of.

Aren't they such great parents?

Caterpillars are larvae of butterflies and moths. They typically molt four or five times before becoming a pupa. The pupa of a moth is covered in a protective cocoon. A butterfly pupa, called a chrysalis, does not have a cocoon covering it.

When you find a caterpillar, put it carefully in your container with a stick so it can eventually climb it to form its pupa. You'll need to keep up a steady supply of fresh food for your caterpillar. It won't eat dry or dead leaves, so you'll need to get it fresh leaves from its host plant every day. Are you a finicky eater, too?

Mist the leaves with your spray bottle so that the caterpillars have moisture. They'll get it from the leaves as they eat. When your caterpillars pupate, your waiting begins.

Usually a pupa will get dark or clear right before the adult butterfly or moth is ready to emerge. Watch carefully because once it begins to emerge, it happens quickly. The adult will crawl out of the chrysalis or cocoon and hang, pumping its wings until they are dry. If your caterpillars were butterfly larvae, then make sure you have some nectar-soaked cotton balls or cut up fruit at the bottom of your jars. They'll need to refuel as soon as their wings are dry.

If you have a moth, check the Internet or a field guide to find out if that species feeds as an adult. Some moths, like the luna moth, only live about four or five days and don't feed at all during that time. You'll want to let it go within a day or two, so that it has time to find a mate and live some of its short life outside in the fresh air.

Other species might be okay to keep for a few extra days so that you can observe them. Remember to let them go at some point, though. Butterflies and moths are meant to flutter in the garden, and you've already created a perfect natural habitat outside.

ADORABLE LIFE CYCLE CRAFT

THERE ARE LOTS OF GREAT BUTTERFLY LIFECYCLE CRAFTS, PROJECTS AND PRINTABLES ON THE INTERNET. I EVEN HAVE A PRINTABLE JOURNAL AND COLORING SHEETS ON MY SITE. HERE'S A SUPER EASY ONE, THOUGH, AND YOU CAN USE THINGS YOU LIKELY HAVE IN YOUR PANTRY RIGHT NOW. GET CREATING!

MATERIALS

Markers

Paper plate

Dried pasta: orzo (5-6), spiral (1), small shell (1), small bowtie (1)

Glue

INSTRUCTIONS

First, bring your materials outside to a table or good crafting space. Divide the paper plate into four quadrants and label them egg, caterpillar, pupa and adult. Draw and color a leaf or plant in the egg quadrant. Glue the orzo pasta onto the leaves in your plant to represent the eggs.

In the caterpillar section, draw a caterpillar munching on some leaves, and color the spiral pasta the same color with which you colored your caterpillar. Glue the pasta onto your caterpillar's back to make it three-dimensional.

In the pupa section, draw a stick and glue the shell pasta to the stick to represent the pupa stage of your butterfly or moth. You can color the shell pasta like you did the spiral pasta if you want to.

Finally, color the bowtie pasta and glue it into the last quadrant, and add a head. This is your adult butterfly or moth.

You can show that this life cycle goes on and on by drawing arrows from one quadrant to the next. Hang this near where you are raising your caterpillars inside to remind you of the stages that butterflies and moths go through.

FUN FACT: **Depending on the species, adult butterflies can live between a week and a year! Some complete week- and month-long migratory treks.**

FUNNIES: WHAT ARE CATERPILLARS AFRAID OF?

DOGERPILLARS!

BECOME A BEAUTIFUL BUTTERFLY

BUTTERFLIES ARE EVERYWHERE, AND NOW'S YOUR CHANCE TO BECOME ONE FOR A LITTLE WHILE. WILL YOU FLUTTER AROUND AND PLAY? OR, WILL YOU DECORATE YOUR WINGS REALISTICALLY AND MIMIC THE MIGRATORY PATH OF MONARCH BUTTERFLIES? WHATEVER YOU DO, HAVE FUN AND PLAY AROUND, IMAGINING THAT YOU'RE A BUTTERFLY ON ITS LONG MIGRATORY FLIGHT.

MATERIALS

Large sheet of poster board

Scissors

Ribbon or yarn, cut into two pieces

Markers, paints, pastels or your favorite art supplies

INSTRUCTIONS

Fold the poster board in half and cut out a wing shape. Decorate the butterfly wings with your art supplies. You can make this realistic by grabbing a butterfly field guide and copying the markings of your favorite butterfly species, or you can have fun and be whimsical, making up patterns and mixing colors as you go.

Once the wings are decorated and dry, punch two holes towards the top, and two towards the middle of your wings. We just used a sharp pencil to poke our holes.

Thread the yarn through the holes to make arm bands (like backpack straps) on the back of the wings, and tie them securely. You can see how we made ours in the photo.

Now, put your wings on and flutter with the butterflies in your yard! Maybe you can even grab a great book about butterfly migration like *An Extraordinary Life* by Laurence Pringle and Bob Marstall, then act it out.

FUN FACT: Butterfly wings are actually transparent, made up of layers of a protein called chitin. Thousands of tiny scales cover those chitin layers, reflecting all the different colors we see. As butterflies get older, the scales fall off and we can see transparent patches on their wings.

SNEAKY SPIDERS

I'm not a huge fan of spiders in my house, but I love looking at them out in the yard.

HOW ABOUT YOU? DO YOU LIKE SPIDERS?

Spiders are not insects. They belong to a group of animals called arachnids (*Arachnida*). Scorpions, ticks and mites are part of the arachnid family too. Arachnids have two body parts, unlike insects that have three. They have eight legs, and do not chew their food.

Spiders actually vomit digestive juices onto, or in the case of some species—into, their prey, and then suck in the liquefied meal. So, digestion takes place outside of the spider's body. Kind of cool, huh? Spiders need their prey to stay super still during this process, so they'll inject a poison into their meal's body, then wrap it in silk and wait until it is mealtime. Then, it will repeat the process of vomiting digestive juices and sucking, over and over again until it is full.

Spiders can make interesting pets, and most can be kept in a small glass or plastic terrarium. If you keep one for a while, you'll be able to watch the cool way it eats for yourself.

FUNNIES:
WHY ARE SPIDERS GOOD SWIMMERS?
THEY HAVE WEBS UNDER THEIR FEET!

A CREEPY-CRAWLY PET
YOUR PARENT WILL NOT LOVE

IT'S REALLY EASY TO MAKE YOUR OWN SPIDER HOME. MAKE SURE YOU ASK IF YOU CAN BRING ONE INTO THE HOUSE THOUGH.
SPIDERS ARE ONE OF THOSE CREATURES THAT ARE INTERESTING, BUT HATED BY MANY PEOPLE.

MATERIALS

Soil or dirt

Small plastic terrarium (critter keeper) from a pet store or a plastic container that has a tight-fitting lid and is well-ventilated with tiny air holes

Leaf litter, sticks and/or pieces of bark

Small piece of sponge in a dish with a bit of water

Petroleum jelly (optional)

INSTRUCTIONS

Head outside to where you can find some dirt for this habitat setup. Spread some soil in a layer on the bottom of your terrarium. Make sure it isn't wet. Spiders prefer their habitats to be dry. Put a layer of twigs, leaf litter, sticks and bark over top of the soil.

Arrange some of the sticks and bark so they are crossed and upright. You want your spider to have places in which to hide and weave their webs.

Place your small dish with the water-soaked sponge in the habitat so your spider has a fresh water source.

Go spider hunting.

Unlike some of the other insects you've handled during the activities in this book, spiders aren't always safe to hold. To make sure you capture a spider carefully, follow these tips:

Grab a jar or other recyclable container with a lid and search your backyard for spider webs or spiders crawling around.

When you find one, gently coax it into your container using the lid.

Dump it into your already prepared terrarium, and place the lid on tightly.

If you want to make sure that your spider spins its web towards the bottom of the terrarium, and not the top or lid (so you can open the enclosure easily for feeding), then spread a thin layer of petroleum jelly around the edge and top of the lid.

Give your spider prey to eat once or twice a week, depending on its size. Simply put a cricket or another insect into the terrarium with it. Watch it feed—it's so fascinating. If it doesn't eat what you put in the terrarium, try other insects of varying sizes until you find things it will eat.

Spiders can make good pets, but if you ever get tired of keeping it, then make sure you release it back to the area in your yard where you found it originally.

SPIDER-FRIENDLY FRAMES

SPIDERS LIKE TO WEAVE THEIR WEBS IN SHELTERED AREAS OF YOUR YARD, USUALLY NEAR PLANTS WHERE INSECTS LIKE TO HANG OUT. AND WHILE THEY SEEM CREEPY TO SOME PEOPLE, SPIDERS ARE AWESOME BACKYARD TENANTS. THEY CAN EAT ALL SORTS OF PESKY BACKYARD PESTS. WITH THIS ACTIVITY, YOU'LL ENCOURAGE THEM TO TAKE UP RESIDENCE IN YOUR YARD.

MATERIALS

Old window panes, picture frames, bike tires or other recyclables that have open frame-like areas

Your Nature Journal (page 12, optional)

INSTRUCTIONS

Make a spider-friendly area in your yard by leaning open recyclables against trees, walls and shrubs.

Check back often. You'll likely find that spiders have taken up residency in your spider shelters within a few days or weeks. You may even want to observe them draw their web designs and jot down your thoughts in your nature journal.

FUN FACT: Tarantulas can fling tiny hairs called urticating hairs at their predators. They have small barbs on them that get in a predator's eyes and nose, irritating the soft tissue so the tarantula can get away. Ouch! They're like miniature porcupines!

SPINNING SENSATIONAL WEBS

SPIDERS ARE PRETTY AMAZING, AREN'T THEY? THEIR SPIDER WEBS ARE AS MUCH AS TEN TIMES THE SIZE OF THEIR BODIES, AND THEY BUILD ONE ALMOST EVERY DAY.

COULD YOU DO THAT? DO YOU THINK YOU COULD BUILD SOMETHING TEN TIMES BIGGER THAN YOURSELF, AND HAVE IT COME OUT AS INTRICATELY DESIGNED AS A SPIDER WEB? IF YOU WERE TO DO THAT, HOW BIG WOULD YOUR WEB NEED TO BE? TRY IT OUT IN THIS SIMPLE ACTIVITY.

MATERIALS

Measuring tape

Yarn

Double-sided tape

INSTRUCTIONS

First, head outside with your materials. Measure your height using your measuring tape, and then calculate how wide your web would have to be. Remember—if you were a spider it would be ten times your height!

Stick one end of your yarn to a tree, and then try to build a web, mimicking the patterns you observed when you went hunting for a web to capture. You'll need a large area. Good luck!

Spiders create their webs by releasing a single thread of silk, just like you're doing with your yarn. The spider starts by sticking its thread to a single point, and then attaches the other end to the starting point.

Amazingly, spiders can spin two types of thread while they build their webs. Some threads are sticky to catch prey, and others are not, so they can easily walk across them.

It's a lot harder than it seems, isn't it? How did you do? Were you able to replicate a spider's web?

Probably not, but it's fun to try things like that. My kids love when we take a skein of inexpensive yarn and make a spider web to play in. We've done it in the house and in the backyard.

Now . . . go find some friends and pretend to be spiders and prey this afternoon! Your web is ready!

FUN FACT: Abandoned spider webs are called cobwebs. Spiders were once nicknamed cobs for the Old English word for spider, *attercops*, which means "poison head."

SENDING SPIDER MESSAGES THROUGH VIBRATIONS

SPIDER EXPERIMENT ONE

HOW QUICKLY DO YOU THINK A SPIDER CAN DETECT PREY ON ITS WEB? THIS IS A COOL WAY TO FIND OUT. YOU'LL USE VIBRATION TO SEND MESSAGES TO A SPIDER IN THE YARD, AND SEE HOW IT REACTS! HOW COOL IS THAT—TALKING TO SPIDERS! YOU CAN BE THE NEXT SPIDER WHISPERER . . . MAYBE EVEN HAVE YOUR OWN REALITY SHOW SOMEDAY . . . TRY IT NOW!

MATERIALS

Metal bar, tuning fork or other object that vibrates when struck

Wooden block

Stopwatch or watch with a second hand

Your Nature Journal (page 12)

INSTRUCTIONS

Look for a web outside in your yard that has a spider on it. Hit your metal bar or tuning fork against the wooden block to set it vibrating and very gently (you don't want to ruin the web) set it against the spider web about 6 inches (15 cm) from the spider. Time how long it takes for the spider to get to the point where you touched.

Write that down in your nature journal.

Experiment with different vibrations. Hit the metal bar harder and softer against the wooden block to change the frequency of the vibration. Each time, let the spider rest, then place the bar 6 inches (15 cm) from where it sits.

Time the spider each time and note whether or not the change in vibration affects how quickly the spider responds.

Why do you think the spider reacts as it does? Those vibrations tell it something— that dinner may have just gotten tangled in its web—and it needs to act fast. Pretty cool! Try it again sometime with a different spider and compare your results.

FUN FACT: Spiders have between two and six spinnerets on the backs of their abdomens. These are like tiny showerheads each with hundreds of holes that spray out liquid silk. It's amazing to think that those tiny showerheads create homes and food traps for arachnids. So super cool!

STUPENDOUS SPIDER WEB ART

EVER SEE A SPIDER WEB IN THE YARD AND WONDER HOW SUCH A BEAUTIFUL PIECE OF ART COULD BE CREATED BY SUCH A TINY CREATURE? THEY'RE AMAZING. AND THE COOL THING IS THAT THEY SPIN NEW WEBS ALL THE TIME, SO YOU CAN CAPTURE ONE TO KEEP FOR YOURSELF TO STUDY FOR PATTERNS. I'LL SHOW YOU HOW!

MATERIALS

Black construction paper

Talcum powder

Hair spray

INSTRUCTIONS

Now, go be a super sleuth outside and find a spider web to capture. Don't disturb a web that has a spider or prey on it. Look for a web that isn't in use. Spiders spin new webs every day or two, though, so don't worry if you accidentally take one that was going to be used.

When you find a good web, gently dust it completely with talcum powder by shaking the container so that the powder comes out in a fine shower—like it's raining on the web. The powder will stick to the web, making the spider silk look white.

Hold your construction paper underneath the web, and slowly bring it upwards towards the web until it detaches from whatever branches it was attached to.

Spray the web with hair spray and set it aside to dry.

Once it's dry, you can further protect it by taking it to an office supply store and having it laminated, or slipping it into a clear plastic sheet protector.

Enjoy your natural artwork!

FUN FACT: It is estimated that there are one million spiders in every acre of land, though it might be closer to three million in the tropics. That means that no human is ever more than 10 feet (3 m) away from a spider. Ever. Does that excite or terrify you?

BACKYARD HERPETOLOGY

(HER-PE-'TÄ-LE-JĒ)

SALAMANDERS, SNAKES, LIZARDS, TOADS, OH MY!

Herpetology is the subfield of biology where scientists study reptiles and amphibians. Its name comes from the Greek word *herpeton*, which means creeping creature. There are over 7,000 different species of amphibians on Earth and over 10,000 species of reptiles currently known.

Most scientists who study herpetology tend to specialize in learning about one specific species, like the scientist I met who specializes in the study of the red-sided garter snake.

I love that there are people out there that study one species of snake for their whole lives! It's fascinating how passionate people can be about things that interest them.

Is there a specific herp (the nickname for reptiles and amphibians) you are interested in learning about? Think about why you want to learn about it, and then go find out all about it!

There's a lot to learn about different reptiles and amphibians, but depending on where you live, you might not be able to find any in your backyard as easily as you could find the bugs, insects and worms in the last chapter. So, while I'll show you how to set up a section of your yard to make it "herp friendly," most of the activities and experiments in this chapter can be done without any animals in hand.

If you do live in a place that has lots of snakes, turtles, frogs and other herps all around, use caution when you're handling them. I love getting outside and catching snakes and tadpoles, but I'm careful to know what species I'll find in my area, and I wash my hands well after I hold them.

YOU SHOULD DO THE SAME.

Reptiles and amphibians are super cool to learn about and observe. If you can, and you don't have them in your backyard, ask an adult to take you hiking or to play near a creek or pond in the spring or summer. There's so much to see!

ROCKIN' REPTILES

DO SNAKES FREAK YOU OUT? How about lizards? Do you think reptiles are cool? Would you want one for a pet?

Shhhh . . . don't tell my son (because he really wants a corn snake for a pet), but I miss the leopard gecko I once had. It was fun to watch and really neat to handle. Many people think that reptiles are slimy, but they're not. They kind of have a bumpy, dry, scaly feel as you hold them.

All reptiles share some common characteristics. They have scales. They lay eggs. They rely on their sense of smell almost exclusively.

Both snakes and lizards rely primarily on their sense of smell when looking for prey. Some snakes, like the nocturnal pit viper, also have heat-sensing organs in their heads that help them locate warm-blooded prey in the dark, along with their sense of smell.

But, while snakes and lizards use their sense of smell to find food, they don't smell with their noses like we do. They smell using their tongues. Let's go learn more!

BASKING BEAUTIES: REPTILES IN THE HEAT

HAVE YOU EVER WONDERED WHY SNAKES AND OTHER REPTILES AND AMPHIBIANS BASK IN THE SUN? WHY THEY COME OUT DURING THE DAY AND HANG OUT ON ROCKS AND LOGS? REPTILES AND AMPHIBIANS ARE ECTOTHERMIC, SO INSTEAD OF USING ENERGY FROM FOOD TO KEEP ITS BODY TEMPERATURE REGULATED LIKE WE DO, A SNAKE USES THE ENVIRONMENT TO WARM ITSELF UP AND COOL ITSELF DOWN.

MANY PEOPLE THINK OF REPTILES AND AMPHIBIANS AS COLD-BLOODED CREATURES, AND WHILE THEIR BLOOD CAN BE COLD AT TIMES, IT CAN ALSO BE QUITE WARM. THAT'S WHY SCIENTISTS PREFER THE TERM ECTOTHERMIC TO DESCRIBE HOW THESE ANIMALS USE THEIR ENVIRONMENT TO REGULATE TEMPERATURES.

WHERE DO YOU THINK THE BEST PLACE WOULD BE FOR A SNAKE OR LIZARD TO BASK DURING THE DAY? HOW ABOUT AFTER THE SUN HAS SET? GRAB YOUR NATURE JOURNAL, GET THE FOLLOWING MATERIALS, AND TRY TO FIND OUT ON THE NEXT SUNNY DAY.

MATERIALS

Dark construction paper

Light construction paper

Aluminum foil

Light colored rock

Dark colored rock

Thermometers (find at your local discount store)

Your Nature Journal (page 12)

INSTRUCTIONS

Take each of the items outside and find a flat, sunny spot, then take each item's temperature with the thermometer and record the starting temperature.

Leave them alone for 10 minutes, then touch them and take their new temperature and record it. Leave the items in the sun for 2 hours, then record their temperature in your journal.

Take them inside and set them back on the table for ten minutes, then record their temperature.

Look over your results and form some conclusions by answering the following questions:

Did all the items warm up and cool down at the same rate?

If you were a snake or a lizard, which of those materials would be the best place to bask on during the day? Why?

Which would be the best place to bask on after the sun has set? Why?

FUNNIES: WHAT DO YOU CALL A SNAKE THAT BUILDS THINGS?
A BOA CONSTRUCTOR!

SNEAKY, SCENT-HUNTING REPTILES

MOST SNAKES SHOOT THEIR TONGUES IN AND OUT, UP AND DOWN, AND PULL THEM BACK INSIDE THEIR MOUTHS WHERE THERE ARE TWO OPENINGS. THESE OPENINGS LEAD TO THE JACOBSON'S ORGAN. SNAKES RUB THEIR TONGUE ON THIS SENSITIVE ORGAN, WIPING OFF THE SCENTS THEY HAVE GATHERED. (MANY LIZARDS SMELL THAT WAY, TOO.)

THE JACOBSON'S ORGAN THEN SENDS A SIGNAL TO THE SNAKE'S BRAIN SO IT CAN IDENTIFY THE SCENT AS PREY, PREDATOR OR MATE. CAN YOU IMAGINE RELYING ON ONLY YOUR SENSE OF SMELL TO FIND FOOD AND FRIENDS? LET'S SEE HOW YOU'D DO. IN THIS GAME, YOU'LL PRETEND TO BE SNAKES.

MATERIALS

Cotton balls

Scented oils or extracts (peppermint, almond, vanilla, etc.)

Plastic zipper-top bags

Permanent marker

Blindfold

Friends to play with

Timer

Your Nature Journal (page 12)

INSTRUCTIONS

Prepare the materials before playing the game, then head outside.

Soak a separate cotton ball in each of the oils or extracts and place them in separate bags and zip them shut.

Choose one of the scents you've already used and soak another cotton ball in that oil, place it in its own bag, seal and write SNAKE on the outside of the bag with the permanent marker. Choose a player to be the snake.

Secure a blindfold on the snake, hand him or her their scented bag, and have the snake familiarize itself with the scent by opening the bag and smelling it.

Have all the other players spread out with a different scented bag, and have them open them up and hold them out in front of their bodies.

Turn on the timer, and let the snake try to find its mate (or friend) by finding the player with the matching scent just by using his or her sense of smell.

Once the snake finds its mate, record its time, mix the scents back up and choose a new snake. Play again, trying to beat the first snake's time.

What did you think about having to rely on your sense of smell to locate your friend? A good scientist writes reflections like these in their nature journal. Take a few minutes and write about what you did during this game and what you thought about it.

Wouldn't it be strange to flick your tongue in and out, rubbing it against holes inside your mouth in order to smell? The animal world really is amazing. And snakes and lizards might just be some of the coolest things in the animal world!

> **FUN FACTS:** Cobras are the most aggressive snakes in the world. They're so dangerous that just one drop of venom could kill 50 humans. Whoa! I'd hate to have a cobra get a whiff of me in its habitat!

WHERE ARE ALL THE REPTILES?

IF REPTILES RELY ON THEIR SENSE OF SMELL TO FIND FOOD, MATES AND TO KNOW WHEN A PREDATOR IS NEARBY, HOW DO YOU THINK THEY PROTECT THEMSELVES FROM THOSE PREDATORS? REPTILES, LIKE SO MANY OTHER CREATURES IN YOUR YARD (AND YES—THERE ARE PROBABLY SNAKES AND LIZARDS IN YOUR YARD FROM TIME TO TIME) USE CAMOUFLAGE TO KEEP THEM SAFE FROM BEING EATEN. THEY'RE SO GOOD AT HIDING THAT I BET YOU'VE RARELY SEEN A SNAKE OR LIZARD IN YOUR YARD—AND IF YOU HAVE, GOOD FOR YOU! THAT'S QUITE AN ACCOMPLISHMENT.

SEE JUST HOW COLORING HELPS SNAKES AND LIZARDS STAY ALIVE WITH THIS SIMPLE GAME USING COLORED OBJECTS TO REPRESENT REPTILES IN YOUR YARD!

MATERIALS

Colored craft sticks or pipe cleaners in different colors

Patch of grass

A friend

Blindfold

Timer

Other places to play—like a driveway, sandbox or garden

Your Nature Journal (page 12)

FUN FACT: Ilha da Queimada Grande, otherwise known as Snake Island, is just off the coast of Brazil and strictly off-limits to humans. Scientists estimate that there are between one and five venomous snakes on every square meter of island terrain. The golden lancehead is a pit viper species responsible for nearly 90 percent of all Brazilian snake deaths every year. And the island is covered with them. Walking on the island means you're never more than three feet (1 m) from a death bite. Yikes!

INSTRUCTIONS

Choose 10 to 15 craft sticks in each color—making sure you have green—then head out to your backyard.

Choose a player to be blindfolded.

Once the blindfold is secure, scatter the sticks across the grass.

Set a timer for 5 minutes, remove your partner's blindfold, and have him or her see how many "reptiles in the grass" they can find before the timer goes off.

Once the timer goes off, sort them by color and count how many of each color your partner found. Did he or she find them all? Which color was easiest to find? Hardest? Why?

Play the game again, but this time *you* try to find the reptiles.

Did you find them all? Was your experience similar to your partner's?

Keep playing the game, but try it out on different surfaces like the driveway, garden, blacktop, etc.

Compare your success rate to your partner's and then compare both success rates between surfaces.

Make sure you find all of the craft sticks you started with before you head inside for the day. It's important to take care of your yard.

A reptile's coloring helps keep them from being found. That's why garter snakes tend to have greenish colors and rattlesnakes tend to be brownish. They need to blend into their unique habitats.

It was probably more difficult for you to find the green sticks in your grass because they blended in just like a garter snake would. Reptiles have amazing adaptations.

RADICAL REPTILES: SNAKE TEMPERATURE REGULATION

SNAKES ARE MASTERS AT REGULATING THEIR BODY TEMPERATURES, OR KEEPING THEMSELVES AT THE PERFECT TEMPERATURE. BESIDES TAKING A DIP IN THE WATER OR MOVING TO A MORE SHADED AREA, THEY CHANGE THE WAY THEY'RE ARRANGING THEIR BODIES IN ORDER TO RELEASE OR PRESERVE HEAT. IN THIS ACTIVITY, YOU'LL SEE HOW DIFFERENT BODY ARRANGEMENTS CAN AFFECT A REPTILE'S BODY TEMPERATURE. GRAB YOUR MATERIALS, HEAD OUTSIDE AND CHECK IT OUT!

MATERIALS

Two small hand towels that are the same color

Two thermometers

Your Nature Journal (page 12)

INSTRUCTIONS

Bring your materials to your backyard on a hot, sunny day. Roll up each of your towels into a tube shape and pop a thermometer into the center of each one. Lay them in a sunny area—one stretched out and one rolled into a coil.

Which do you think will warm up the fastest? Write your hypothesis in your nature journal.

Draw a simple chart in your journal with three columns like the one below. One should be labeled Straight Snake and the other should be labeled Coiled Snake. Record the temperature of each snake every minute. You'll want to note which snake reaches a maximum temperature the quickest (you'll know this because the temperature will stop rising each time you check it). How long does it take for the other snake to reach that temperature? You may need more rows than the sample table.

TIME ELAPSED	STRAIGHT SNAKE	COILED SNAKE
1 Minute		
2 Minutes		
3 Minutes		
4 Minutes		
5 Minutes		
6 Minutes		
7 Minutes		

(continued)

Once they reach the same temperature, move them to a shady spot, but keep them either stretched out or coiled. Record their temperature every minute. Which cools faster?

While a snake stretches out to absorb the sun's energy more quickly than when it's coiled, it will coil up to conserve that energy and stay warm for longer.

Sometimes, though, stretching out or coiling up isn't enough to keep a snake warm. During winter months, snakes enter a brumation period, which is similar to hibernation. They just can't keep their body temperature up enough to be actively out in the wild during the colder months.

Brumation is different than hibernation because snakes, and other reptiles that brumate, don't go completely to sleep. They eat a lot less, sometimes not eating at all for months, but still need to rouse themselves to find water to drink. Brumation, like hibernation, is triggered by falling temperatures and a decrease in daylight hours.

FUN FACT: Some snake species, like the red-sided garter snake, come together in large numbers to keep each other warm through the winter months. At the Narcisse Snake Dens in Manitoba, Canada, you can see, touch and interact with tens of thousands of red-sided garter snakes all together in one place. Amazing!

CREATING LOUNGING SPACES FOR LIZARDS

LIKE ALL ECTOTHERMIC ANIMALS, LIZARDS RELY ON THE SUN AND AIR TO KEEP THEIR BODY TEMPERATURES REGULATED. BECAUSE OF THIS, LIZARDS NEED BASKING AREAS THAT ARE SAFE FOR THEM TO RELAX AND SOAK UP THE SUN'S HEAT. ROCK PILES AND WALLS ARE WONDERFUL AREAS IN WHICH TO WATCH OUT FOR THESE NEAT CREATURES.

THEY'RE REALLY THE PERFECT HABITAT FOR LIZARDS BECAUSE THEY CAN GET WARM AND THEY HAVE THE LITTLE CREVICES BETWEEN THE ROCKS TO DART INTO AND HIDE IF PREDATORS COME. YOU CAN MAKE ONE YOURSELF!

MATERIALS

20- to 24-inch (50- to 60-cm) diameter terra cotta pot

Rocks of various shapes and sizes

Cinder blocks

Bricks

Your Nature Journal (page 12)

INSTRUCTIONS

Create the perfect place for a lizard to take up residence by filling your clay pot with different shaped rocks, leaving gaps and cracks between them. Set it up in your backyard near bushes, walls and other spots that are lit up with streaky patches of sunlight during the day. They'll sun themselves in the patches of light, but enjoy the variety of shade and shadows to hide in if they sense danger. Scatter cinder blocks, bricks and more rocks in a jumbled pile so there are lots of hiding places for lizards to get away from predators.

Check it out every few days to see if there are any signs of lizards living there. On hot, sunny days, you can sit out in the yard with your nature journal and quietly observe. If you see a lizard or even a snake sunning itself on the rocks, sketch them in your journal, then look it up to see which species visit your yard.

MORE FUN: Many lizards can let go of their tail to distract predators and escape. This is called tail autonomy.

AWESOME AMPHIBIANS

HAVE YOU EVER CAUGHT A FROG OR A TOAD? My kids love playing in ponds and creeks, and seeing if they can find toads in our backyard. They're probably one of the easiest herps to find and catch.

Do you know the difference between the two? Many people don't. While they belong to the same group, they're actually quite different.

Frogs need to live near the water to keep their smooth skin moist. They have narrow bodies with high, rounded eyes. They have many predators and can take long, high jumps using their muscular back legs.

Toads don't need to live near the water to survive. They stay moist by digging into the dirt. They are easier to find in backyards that don't have water sources. Their skin is rough, dry and bumpy, and they give off a bitter taste and smell when they're threatened.

Their bodies are wider than frogs and they have lower, football-shaped eyes. They take short hops because their back legs aren't as powerful as a frog's and they're a lot shorter.

They're both fun to observe and easy to catch, so be on the lookout and enjoy finding these hoppy amphibians. Most of the activities focus on catching toads, though, since they're not so dependent on a water source. They might be easier to find in a backyard.

TOAD-ALLY TUBULAR TOAD HOUSE

WHEN YOU ARE SEARCHING FOR BACKYARD AMPHIBIANS, TOADS ARE EASY TO ATTRACT. THEY EAT THOUSANDS OF INSECTS FROM VEGETABLE GARDENS AND FLOWER BEDS, SO THEY'RE GREAT TO HAVE AROUND, TOO.

WITH THIS FUN PROJECT, IT'S EASY TO TURN OLD OR BROKEN FLOWER POTS INTO TOAD HOUSES. YOU CAN USE THINGS LIKE COFFEE CANS, TOO.

MATERIALS

Flowerpot or coffee can

Nature treasures like pebbles, rocks and sticks

Glue gun

Small shovel

Dried leaves

Dish with water (optional)

INSTRUCTIONS

Bring your materials to a table in the backyard, and take some time to decorate the outside of your flowerpot or coffee can. Pebbles, rocks, sticks and other natural treasures are great for this. Just attach them with a glue gun.

Pick out a cool, shady spot in your yard and dig a hole. Set your container on its side, half buried in the hole. Toads love burrowing, so a dirt floor will encourage them to call the toad house their new home.

Crumble up some of the dried leaves on top of the dirt for bedding, and wait for your new residents. You can further encourage toads to live there by keeping out a dish of water so there is a readily available water source.

FUNNIES: WHY ARE TOADS SO HAPPY ALL THE TIME?
THEY EAT WHAT BUGS THEM!

KEEPING TOADS AS PETS

HAVE YOU EVER WANTED TO KEEP A TOAD AS A PET? IT'S TOAD-ALLY EASY TO DO, AND IF YOU TAKE GOOD CARE OF IT, YOUR TOAD CAN BE A GREAT PET FOR YEARS. WE HAVE TWO RIGHT NOW, AND THEY HOP OUT OF THEIR HIDING PLACES WHEN MY DAUGHTER APPROACHES THEIR HABITAT WITH FOOD. SUPER AWESOME PETS!

WHEN YOU'RE LOOKING FOR TOADS TO KEEP AS PETS, GO OUTSIDE JUST BEFORE DARK. THE BUGS ARE OUT, AND TOADS ARE JUST BECOMING ACTIVE. LOOK AROUND WOOD PILES AND BEHIND ROCKS. CATCH A TOAD WITH YOUR HANDS OR THE NET YOU MADE ON PAGE 17.

MATERIALS

Old tank or aquarium, large plastic box or other large container

Dirt or peat moss

Small terra cotta pot and saucer

Water

INSTRUCTIONS

A toad habitat is easy to set up. Bring your materials to a good workspace outside. You'll need an old aquarium or another large container that has a screened lid. You can make one by laying an old screen on top of a large plastic shoebox.

Toads like moist dirt, and they like to dig, so put a few inches (6 to 7 cm) of dirt or peat moss on the bottom of your tank while you're outside setting it up. Partially bury a terra cotta saucer for water. Lay the terra cotta pot on its side in the corner and layer the bottom with more dirt or moss. This will give your toad a place to hide when it needs to.

Put your toad gently in the aquarium and set the lid on tightly. You'll need to feed your toad every other day. And, since toads don't like to eat the same things over and over again, you'll want to change things up. Catch flies to give it, dig up earthworms, find mealworms . . . there are lots of things in your backyard to feed your toad.

FUN FACT: **Did you know that a group of toads is called a knot? I never knew that!**

CREATING A SALAMANDER-FRIENDLY SPACE

THERE ARE MORE AMPHIBIANS THAN JUST FROGS AND TOADS. SALAMANDERS ARE TRICKY AMPHIBIANS TO FIND IN OUR AREA. MY KIDS LOVE GOING TO A VERNAL POOL NEARBY ON THE FIRST WARM RAIN OF THE SPRING TO WATCH SPOTTED SALAMANDERS MIGRATE TO LAY THEIR EGGS. IT'S A PRETTY AMAZING SIGHT. VERNAL POOLS ARE POND-LIKE POOLS OF WATER THAT ARE ONLY IN PLACE FROM EARLY SPRING TO THE MIDDLE OF SUMMER, WHEN THEY EVAPORATE FROM THE HEAT. THEY ARE HOME TO INCREDIBLE CREATURES LIKE SALAMANDERS WHO RELY ON THESE TEMPORARY POOLS FOR SURVIVAL.

YOU CAN ATTRACT SOME OF THE LESS FINICKY SALAMANDERS TO YOUR YARD (ALONG WITH SNAKES AND ARBOREAL [TREE] LIZARDS) PRETTY EASILY.

MATERIALS

Sticks, logs, rocks, etc.

Your Nature Journal (page 12)

INSTRUCTIONS

Like you did with your lizard habitat (page 119), find a place in your yard that has low bushes, a wall or a shady spot. Build up a brush and rock pile.

Pile the logs, sticks and rocks at the base of your wall or bush, and leave lots of cracks and hiding places. Leave it alone for a few weeks. Then, check back to see if you can spot some cool new wildlife in your yard. This is a good time for you to practice your observation skills and watch the pile, while drawing what you see in your nature journal.

FUN FACT: The name salamander comes from Greek and means fire lizard. They got their name when logs were thrown on a fire, and these teeny lizard-like creatures scurried out.

AMPHIBIAN ATHLETICS

FROGS AND TOADS ARE FUN TO PLAY WITH, AS LONG AS YOU ARE REMEMBERING THAT THEY'RE LIVING CREATURES, AND YOU'RE CAREFUL TO TREAT THEM WELL. MY KIDS HAVE ALWAYS LOVED TO RACE THEIR FROGS. IT'S SIMPLE TO SET UP A FROG OR TOAD RACE. COME ON! I'LL SHOW YOU HOW!

MATERIALS

Long plastic container

Several frogs or toads

Friends

INSTRUCTIONS

Set your plastic container on a sturdy outdoor surface like your driveway. This will be your racetrack.

Sit at the start line (one side of the container) with your friends and their frogs or toads, and set them down at the same time. See which one makes it to the other end first. You can encourage your frog or toad to jump by tapping its behind gently.

MORE FUN: Frog races and frog jumping contests were once a famous pastime, even being a part of county fairs everywhere. Look to see if your local county fair has frog jumping contests and how you train a frog to enter. Who knows? You just might discover a new sport!

SCURRYING, SCAVENGING TADPOLES

IF YOU HEAD OUT TO A CREEK OR A POND DURING LATE SPRING AND EARLY SUMMER, YOU'LL PROBABLY SEE LOTS OF TADPOLES SWIMMING AT THE EDGE OF THE WATER—ESPECIALLY IF YOU HEAD THERE IN THE HEAT OF THE DAY. TAKE SOME TIME BEFORE YOU GO, AND PREPARE A HABITAT FOR THEM AT HOME BECAUSE TADPOLES ARE VERY EASY TO RAISE, AND SO FUN TO WATCH AS THEY GO THROUGH THEIR LIFE CYCLE. LET'S GO HUNTING!

MATERIALS

Large container

Gravel

Water pump (optional)

Large, flat rocks

Tadpoles

Your Nature Journal (page 12)

Lettuce, algae, pond plants

FUNNIES: WHAT IS A FROG'S FAVORITE SUMMERTIME TREAT?
HOPSICLES!

INSTRUCTIONS

Get a large container and head out to your backyard. My kids use a 2½-gallon (9 L) aquarium that we ordered online. You can use jars, bins and other containers, too. Just make sure that you have enough room for the tadpoles to move around.

Cover the bottom with gravel or small rocks. Your tadpoles will scavenge for algae in between them. My kids like to add a pump to their tank and bury the line in the gravel. It's not absolutely necessary, but if you have a pump lying around from an old fish tank, it can help keep the water full of oxygen. Otherwise, you should give the water a stir to aerate it a few times each day.

Take your big rocks and arrange them in a pile on one side. Try to get the top rock positioned at a slant. When the tadpoles begin developing their legs, they'll need to be able to crawl out of the water and bask.

Fill your tank with water that's non-chlorinated or a bucket of pond water that you bring home with you when you catch your tadpoles. Your tank is ready, so add your tadpoles in whenever you find them. You can also add frog or toad spawn, or eggs, if you find that instead. Just lay the jelly-like spawn at the top of the water.

We keep our tadpoles in the kitchen so my kids can watch them all day long. They use their nature journals to draw pictures as they change from tadpole to frog. It's so much fun.

Frogs take between six and twelve weeks to go through metamorphosis, so be patient! Use your nature journal to record observations as they grow. You'll need to feed your hungry tadpoles often. Ours like boiled lettuce. We boil dark green lettuce for ten to twelve minutes and let it cool. Sometimes we lay a leaf right on the top of the water and watch them eat. Other times we chop it up and freeze it in little clumps to feed them each day. When the frogs and toads are fully developed into froglets and toadlets, bring them back to the place where you caught them and let them go.

BACKYARD ORNITHOLOGY

(ÔR-NE-'THÄ-LE-JĒ)

BIRDS, BIRDS AND MORE BIRDS

Ornithology is the study of birds, and is an area of science where everyday people—just like you—can make important contributions and discoveries. There are annual bird counts around the world, and kids and adults help by counting the different species they see in their yards so scientists know where to go to study certain species.

Ornithologists study everything there is to know about birds, and most specialize in one aspect of that. So, you might find some ornithologists study how different parts of a bird work and how those body systems work together. You might find one who is interested in one specific species and its migratory path.

There are some really cool things to discover about birds and they're super easy to study from your own backyard. You'll make some feeders to encourage new birds to visit, and observe their preferences! It's so much fun to have a nature-friendly place right in your yard.

FUN FACT: A bird's eyes take up about 50 percent of its head, while ours only take up about 5 percent. If our eyes took up that much space, they'd be the size of baseballs!

POPPED CORN, UNPOPPED CORN
BIRD EXPERIMENT ONE

MANY PEOPLE HANG BIRD FEEDERS OR SCATTER SEED IN THEIR YARD TO ATTRACT BIRDS. DO YOU? WE'LL MAKE SOME DIFFERENT TYPES OF BIRD FEEDERS LATER IN THIS CHAPTER. FOR NOW, LET'S SEE SOME BIRD ETHOLOGY (OR STUDY SOME BIRD BEHAVIOR).

BIRDS LIKE TO EAT SEEDS LIKE SUNFLOWER AND CORN. SOME PEOPLE ENJOY SUNFLOWER SEEDS AND CORN, TOO, BUT THEY TEND TO PREFER THEIR SEEDS TOASTED AND THE CORN ROASTED OR POPPED, NOT RAW. DO YOU THINK BIRDS WOULD LIKE THEIR CORN POPPED LIKE PEOPLE EAT IT? LET'S SEE IF THEY HAVE A PREFERENCE.

MATERIALS

Your Nature Journal (page 12)

Two plastic dishes

Popped corn

Unpopped corn

INSTRUCTIONS

Make a hypothesis in your journal. Do you think that birds will prefer their corn popped or unpopped? Why?

Place your two dishes outside in a safe place near where you've seen birds or already have a feeder set up.

Put popped popcorn on one and unpopped popcorn on the other. It's best if you can observe this experiment from far away. Birds can be skittish, and you don't want to discourage them from enjoying their snack. You can further encourage them to come near enough to the popcorn to eat by sprinkling some of the seed you already know they love around the area where you've placed your plates.

Which did the birds in your area prefer? Mine preferred the popped corn when we tried this most recently, but in the past, they've eaten the unpopped as well. Watching the behaviors of animals like birds is so interesting because we see that they have unique personalities too!

FUN FACT: Many birds kept as pets, including doves, parakeets and lovebirds, enjoy living in pairs for companionship. Do you have a pet bird?

THE SWEET SOUND OF BIRDSONG

BIRDSONG IS IMPORTANT IF BIRDS WANT TO SURVIVE. IT TELLS OTHERS WHAT SPECIES IT IS. IT ANNOUNCES WHETHER IT IS MALE OR FEMALE. IT SCARES INTRUDERS AWAY FROM A NEST.

BIRDS CAN SING DIFFERENT SONGS JUST LIKE INSTRUMENTS CAN PRODUCE DIFFERENT NOTES. EACH ONE TELLS A DIFFERENT STORY. INTERESTINGLY, BIRDS DON'T HAVE A LARYNX LIKE PEOPLE DO. THEY HAVE A BONY STRUCTURE CALLED A SYRINX FOR MAKING SOUNDS. THIS IS CONTROLLED BY SPECIAL MUSCLES THAT VIBRATE TO MAKE DIFFERENT SONGS AND CALLS.

SEE IF YOU CAN LISTEN TO AND RECORD SOME OF THE BIRD SONGS IN YOUR YARD WITH THIS ACTIVITY!

MATERIALS

Digital recorder (from a phone or tablet works well, too)

Field guides and Internet access

Your Nature Journal (page 12)

INSTRUCTIONS

Find a spot in the backyard where a lot of birds hang out like low hanging trees, bushes and shrubs. Secure your recorder near a nest or feeder. Now, go sit somewhere a bit away from the recorder where you can watch without disturbing the birds' activity.

Close your eyes, be very still and listen for several minutes.

Write down the sounds of the birds that you hear in your journal. Try to replicate those sounds as closely as you can. For example, a chickadee makes a chick-a-dee-dee-dee sound. Spend as long as you can, quietly listening and recording the sounds that you hear. You might even want to sketch some pictures of the birds you see in the journal, too, or make notes of what they look like.

When you're finished, use bird books, the Internet, your sound recordings and your notes to identify the birds that you saw and heard. Write the common names of the birds you hear in your journal near your written interpretations of their sounds. Keep a running list of birds you see and hear in your yard in your journal.

> **MORE FUN:** There are lots of birdsongs recorded online. With an adult's permission, find some clips of birds that are local to you. Listen to them and get to know their songs. Then, go to the yard and close your eyes, trying to figure out what birds are around you.

EXPLORING FEATHERS

EVERY BIRD HAS FEATHERS—THEY'RE VERY IMPORTANT TO A BIRD'S SURVIVAL. THEY PROVIDE INSULATION, KEEPING THE BIRD WARM. THEY ALSO ALLOW BIRDS TO FLY BECAUSE THEY HAVE A HOLLOW SHAFT IN THE CENTER THAT GIVES STRUCTURE WITHOUT ADDING WEIGHT.

EACH SHAFT HAS A VANE MADE UP OF MANY BARBS PROJECTING FROM IT. THESE BARBS CLING TO EACH OTHER USING THEIR BARBULES. FEATHERS ARE FASCINATING STRUCTURES. AS YOU OBSERVE THEM IN THIS ACTIVITY, NOTE HOW THESE SEEMINGLY SIMPLE OBJECTS ARE AMAZING EXAMPLES OF NATURE'S WONDER. LOOK CLOSELY AND DRAW WHAT YOU SEE IN YOUR JOURNAL!

MATERIALS

Your Nature Journal (page 12)

Feather (if you can't find one in your yard, the feathers you can find at craft stores make a great substitution)

Magnifying glass (and a microscope if you have it)

Scissors

INSTRUCTIONS

Bring your materials outside and record observations in your nature journal by drawing what you see as you study the feather and all its parts.

Using the magnifying glass, examine the feather from top to bottom. Carefully cut through the center shaft of the feather. What do you notice? How does this help flight?

Look carefully through your magnifying glass at the surface of the feather. What do you notice about the vane? If you have a microscope, look more closely at the barbs that make up the vane of the feather.

Brush backwards against the barbs to separate them. Look through your magnifying glass. How might this affect flight?

While looking through the magnifying glass, smooth the barbs back into place. Do you see the tiny hooks called barbules catching each other to keep the feather in this smooth state?

Feathers are important for different things besides flight. They also help birds show off to attract a mate, keep warm, stay dry or to blend into their surroundings.

FUNNIES: DID YOU HEAR THE JOKE ABOUT THE BROKEN EGG?
YES! IT CRACKED ME UP!

FINDING AND IDENTIFYING BIRD NESTS

BIRDS ARE AMAZING ENGINEERS. THEY CREATE INTRICATELY WOVEN HOMES OUT OF HARD MATERIALS LIKE TWIGS AND BARK. THEY MAKE THEIR HOMES AMONG BRANCHES THAT TWIST AND TURN IN HEAVY WINDS.

THESE HOMES COME IN ALL SHAPES AND SIZES, TOO. FROM THE TINY PING-PONG BALL SIZED NEST OF A HUMMINGBIRD TO THE TEN-FOOT (3-M) WIDE NESTS OF BALD EAGLES, BIRDS CAN BUILD INCREDIBLE STRUCTURES. SEE IF YOU CAN DISCOVER HOW THEY DO IT BY CAREFULLY DISSECTING A NEST IN THIS ACTIVITY.

MATERIALS

Binoculars

Bird's nest

Your Nature Journal (page 12)

Tweezers

Magnifying glass

INSTRUCTIONS

In the late fall or early winter, go outside with your binoculars and search for abandoned bird nests. Most birds migrate and abandon their nests during this time of year, so it's a great time to find unused nests. You can find them in lower branches of trees, shrubs and even among rocks and tall grasses. If the nest you find is up high, ask a grown-up to help you get it down.

Gently take the nest from the tree after you've made sure that it is no longer occupied. Set up a workspace at home in your yard that has room for you to spread out. Make sure you have your nature journal opened up so you can draw what you're doing.

Use your tweezers to separate the pieces of material making up the nest. Examine them closely with your magnifying glass and separate the materials into like piles.

Make a list of materials and analyze how the nest was constructed. Was there a pattern to the materials used? Did the materials give you any clues as to when the nest was built or where the bird flew to gather supplies? Write down any of these observations in your journal.

MORE FUN: Save scraps of colorful yarn and ribbon throughout the year from your craft projects. Hang it from trees in recycled strawberry cartons or in suet bird feeder cages in the springtime. Birds will pull the pieces out and use them in their nests, and you'll be able to see them when you hunt for abandoned nests next fall.

BECOME A FEATHERED ARCHITECT

BIRDS BUILD THEIR NESTS EVERYWHERE, FROM THE TOPS OF SOME TREES TO DITCHES ON THE SIDE OF THE ROAD. SOME SHORE BIRDS EVEN BUILD NESTS OF ROCKS SURROUNDING A CLUTCH OF EGGS. OTHERS BUILD INTRICATE WOVEN CUPS OF GRASSES, TWIGS AND DOWN.

THINK ABOUT THE BIRD NESTS YOU'VE SEEN OR THE ONE YOU RECENTLY DISSECTED. COULD YOU DO IT? COULD YOU BUILD A SECURE NEST FROM MATERIALS YOU FIND IN YOUR YARD? HOW DO BIRDS MAKE IT SEEM SO EASY? LET'S SEE IF YOU'RE AS TALENTED AS THE BIRDS IN YOUR YARD!

MATERIALS

Twigs

Leaves

Dried grass or plants

Paper scraps

Yarn

String

Your Nature Journal (page 12)

INSTRUCTIONS

Walk around the neighborhood, take a hike in the woods or search the Internet to find bird nests of all shapes and sizes. Observe them carefully and try to discover how the nests have been constructed. If you are looking at real nests, try not to disturb any bird families.

Gather a variety of materials from the list, and any additional nest-building supplies you think would be useful, then head outside to get building.

Using just your fingers—no glue or tape—try to build a nest that mimics one of the nests you observed. Make sure your nest would be able to hold two or three eggs.

How did you do? Are you a master nest builder? Or is that task for the birds? Write about your experience and thoughts in your journal.

FUN FACT: The smallest bird egg belongs to the hummingbird and is the size of a pea. The largest bird egg belongs to the ostrich and is the size of a cantaloupe. Wow!

POINTY BEAKS, STUBBY BEAKS
BIRD EXPERIMENT TWO

YOU CAN TELL A LOT ABOUT BIRDS JUST BY LOOKING AT THEIR BEAKS. BEAKS COME IN DIFFERENT SIZES AND SHAPES BECAUSE THEY DO DIFFERENT JOBS. INSECT-EATING BIRDS, LIKE THE BLUEBIRD, HAVE POINTED BEAKS WITH LARGE MOUTHS. CARDINALS AND OTHER SEED-EATERS HAVE A STUBBY, SHARP BEAK. WORM-EATERS LIKE THE ROBIN HAVE POINTED BEAKS FOR DIGGING. WOODPECKERS HAVE A LONG, THIN BEAK THAT IS PERFECT FOR DRILLING INTO TREES.

IN THIS GAME, BECOME A SPARROW OR A SWALLOW, AND USE YOUR BEAK TO EAT YOUR FOOD. NOTICE HOW IMPORTANT IT IS TO HAVE THE RIGHT TOOLS FOR THE JOB!

MATERIALS

A friend

Paper clip

Dried fruit

Clothespin

Nuts

Timer

Your Nature Journal (page 12)

INSTRUCTIONS

You need a friend, parent or sibling to play this game with. Head outside and set up your game.

Stretch the paperclip out so that one end is straight and the other is still bent. This is the sparrow beak. Put the bowl of fruit in front of the player using the paperclip sparrow beak. The other player is the swallow, and is using the clothespin as a beak. Place the bowl of nuts in front of the swallow player.

Set the timer for 3 minutes. Each player tries to get as much food out of their bowl as they can using only their beak. When the time is up, compare the food each player was able to remove from their bowl.

The player with the most bird food in front of them is the winner.

Was the challenge of removing your food easy or difficult? Why do you think that is? Write your thoughts in your journal.

Try the game again, this time switching food. The sparrow should have the nuts and the swallow should have the fruit. Will this change the results of the game? How?

Sparrows in the wild have thick beaks to eat seeds and nuts, while swallows have thin beaks to eat soft creatures like insects. So, in the game, the paperclip is the perfect beak with which to spear soft insects like the soft pieces of dried fruit and the clothespin is perfect for pinching and picking up seeds and nuts.

FUNNIES: WHY DID THE BIRD GO TO THE DOCTOR?
IT WAS SICK AND NEEDED TWEETMENT.

OIL-SLICKED FEATHERS
BIRD EXPERIMENT THREE

WHAT DO YOU THINK WILL HAPPEN IF A BIRD GETS WET? WHEN THE FEATHER IS SMOOTHED, IT CREATES A SOLID WALL TO PUSH AGAINST THE AIR. WHEN THE BARBS ARE MESSED UP, THERE ARE HOLES FOR THE AIR TO COME THROUGH, MAKING IT TOUGH FOR A BIRD TO FLY.

WHEN A BIRD GETS WET, THE WATER ROLLS RIGHT OFF THAT SOLID WALL. THAT'S WHY DUCKS ARE ABLE TO SWIM ALL DAY, BUT TAKE OFF QUICKLY IF THEY'RE THREATENED. BUT, IF OIL GETS ON A DUCK'S FEATHERS, THEY CAN'T DO THEIR JOB NOW—JUST LIKE IF THERE ARE HOLES WHILE THEY'RE FLYING.

TAKE A NEW FEATHER AND SEE FOR YOURSELF HOW OIL CAN HURT BIRDS—ESPECIALLY DUCKS. YOU CAN MAKE OBSERVATIONS AND DRAWINGS IN YOUR NATURE JOURNAL.

MATERIALS

Feathers

Magnifying glass (and a microscope if you have one)

Water

Paper towels

Pipettes or medicine droppers

Cooking oil

Plastic gloves

Dish detergent

Your Nature Journal (page 12)

INSTRUCTIONS

Set up your outdoor workspace. Choose one feather and study it carefully. Look at it under the microscope or magnifying glass and notice how the barbs overlap. This provides a waterproofing effect for the bird.

Dip your feather in a glass of water. Pull it out and look carefully. What happened? Did the water soak in? Bead up? Roll off? Dry your feather by pulling it through a paper towel gently. How quickly did it dry? Write your answers in your journal.

Now, use a pipette or a medicine dropper to add a few drops of oil to the water. Put on your gloves and dip your feather again. Pull it out and look carefully. What happened? What did the oil do to the surface of the feather? Dry your feather by pulling it through a paper towel gently. Does the oil come off? How does the feather look now?

Try to find the best way to clean oily feathers. Dip two more feathers in oil. Clean one with cold water, one with hot water and one in soapy water. Which substance do you think will clean the oil off the best? Why? Write down your hypothesis before you begin.

Which one worked best? The dish soap is able to cut through the oil and get the feather the cleanest. Environmentalists who clean up large scale oil spills often use dish soap to bathe the wildlife that gets trapped in the spill.

EGG-CELLENT CHEMISTRY
BIRD EXPERIMENT FOUR

DO YOU KNOW WHAT A BIRD'S EGGSHELL IS MADE UP OF? BIRD EGGS ARE MADE UP OF A HARD CALCIUM CARBONATE SHELL. ON THE MEMBRANE THAT SURROUNDS THE YOLK AND ALBUMEN INSIDE THE EGG, THERE ARE POINTS WHERE COLUMNS OF CALCITE FORM. THESE COLUMNS CONTINUE TO FORM SIDE BY SIDE UNTIL A SHELL IS MADE. THE SHELL DOES NOT GET HARD UNTIL IT REACHES THE AIR RIGHT BEFORE IT LEAVES THE BIRD'S BODY. CALCITE IS A FORM OF CALCIUM CARBONATE AND THE NECESSARY INGREDIENT FOR FORMING HARD EGGS.

IT'S POSSIBLE TO REMOVE THE CALCIUM CARBONATE AND HAVE THE EGG STAY INTACT THROUGH A SIMPLE CHEMICAL REACTION USING SIMPLE WHITE VINEGAR. HAVE YOU EVER MADE A NAKED EGG BEFORE? TRY IT NOW!

MATERIALS

Chicken eggs (you'll want several in case any break, and so you can have a control)

Two large glass jars

Water

Vinegar

Corn syrup

Your Nature Journal (page 12)

Food coloring

INSTRUCTIONS

Bring the materials outside and set up your workspace for the experiment. Put one egg in a jar of water. This will be the control egg to remind you what the egg was like at the beginning of the experiment.

Place another egg in a jar of vinegar. What's happening? Jot down your observations in your nature journal. For the best results, you'll want to leave the egg in the original vinegar for 24 hours, then carefully drain the old vinegar out and re-cover the egg with fresh vinegar. Leave that alone for a week.

What happened? You should have seen a chemical reaction almost immediately. The vinegar started bubbling around the egg's shell. Those bubbles are carbon dioxide. The vinegar is made up of acetic acid and water. The acetic acid in the vinegar reacted with the calcium carbonate in the eggshell.

This made calcium acetate along with the water and carbon dioxide bubbles you saw on the surface of the egg. That reaction left behind only the semi-permeable membrane covering of the egg.

After a few days, take the egg out and carefully handle it. What do you notice? Draw and describe your observations in your nature journal. Try bouncing it gently on the table.

The egg is slightly bigger than it was because that membrane is semi-permeable, meaning that water can pass through it. The process of osmosis is a natural process that works to keep things balanced. There was more water outside the membrane in the vinegar than inside the egg, so through osmosis water passed into the egg, swelling it but making it balanced with the water molecules outside the egg.

What do you think would happen if the egg were in a solution that had a lower concentration of water than what was inside the egg?

(continued)

Since the process of osmosis works to balance systems out, water should pass back out through the membrane into the other solution, shrinking the egg.

Try it—rinse the vinegar off the egg and place it in a cup of corn syrup and let it sit overnight. Did it work? Do you now have a smaller egg?

That hard shell is an important part of what keeps a baby bird developing and healthy while it grows inside its egg. It covers that semi-permeable layer so harmful chemicals and liquids can't get inside.

MORE FUN: There are lots of ways to extend this activity and have more fun with naked eggs.

Try putting the egg back into colored water after it has gotten smaller in the corn syrup. Does the color travel through the membrane into the egg?

Make a new naked egg. Try bouncing it from a few inches (6 to 7 cm) above your patio or driveway (covered in a cloth). Keep holding it farther and farther away from the ground. From how high can you drop it before it breaks rather than bounces?

Ask a question, make a hypothesis and test it. Here are some ideas to get you started: Do organic eggs react more or less than non-organic eggs? Are brown eggs less reactive than white? How do eggs react in different liquids?

FUNNIES: WHAT DO YOU CALL A BIRD IN WINTER?
BRRRRRRRRRRR-D

BLUE FEEDER, GREEN FEEDER
BIRD EXPERIMENT FIVE

LIKE MOST ANIMALS, BIRDS HAVE EYES WITH TWO TYPES OF CELLS. THESE ARE CALLED RODS AND CONES. RODS HELP THEM SEE LIGHT. CONES HELP THEM SEE COLOR. BIRDS HAVE MORE RODS THAN CONES, BUT DON'T HAVE ANY BLOOD VESSELS IN THEIR EYES. THIS HELPS PREVENT SHADOWS AND THE SCATTERING OF LIGHT AS IT ENTERS THE EYE. IMAGES ENTER WITHOUT BEING DIFFUSED AND BIRDS' EYES ARE ABLE TO GET TO WORK PROCESSING LIGHT AND COLORS.

HUMANS HAVE THREE TYPES OF CONES, EACH ABLE TO SEE A SPECIFIC COLOR. WHEN THE CONES COMBINE, WE SEE ALL THE COLORS IN OUR WORLD. BIRDS, THOUGH, HAVE FOUR TYPES OF CONES. SOME EVEN HAVE FIVE! BESIDES THESE COLORS, THEY CAN ALSO SEE ULTRAVIOLET LIGHT, WHICH IS INVISIBLE TO HUMANS. THIS MEANS THAT BIRDS CAN SEE RED, GREEN AND BLUE LIKE WE DO, BUT THEY CAN ALSO SEE TWO ADDITIONAL COLORS. AMAZING!

WITH THEIR SPECIAL COLOR-DETECTION ABILITY, IT WOULD BE INTERESTING TO SEE IF ONE COLOR IS MORE APPEALING TO BIRDS THAN ANOTHER. TRY THIS EXPERIMENT TO FIND OUT!

MATERIALS

Four small wooden or wire bird feeders, unpainted

Squirrel cones or feeder poles (optional)

Paint in 3 colors (red, blue and green)

Large bag of birdseed or bird suet

Scale

Your Nature Journal (page 12)

INSTRUCTIONS

Find a place in your yard to hang the birdfeeders clustered near each other, taking precautions against squirrels. (Hang them on poles or trees with squirrel cones or some other type of deterrent.) Fill them with seed, and leave them for a one to two week period so birds recognize the feeders as a food source and begin to frequent the location.

Following the initial feeding period, take your feeders down and paint three of them—each a different color. Leave the fourth unpainted.

Do you think color will matter to the birds? If so, which color do you think will be most attractive? Why? Write your hypothesis in your nature journal.

Fill each feeder to the top with seed and weigh each, recording the weight in your journal. Date all entries in your journal. Put your feeders back out for 48 hours, then bring them back in and weigh them. Record the weight and refill each.

Weigh the feeders again and record the new full weights. Replace the feeders outside and leave them for another 48 hours. Repeat the procedures every two days for two weeks.

After two weeks, subtract each end weight from the start weight and average the amount of birdseed eaten from each feeder over a two-day period. Remember that to find an average, you add the amounts eaten all together, then divide that answer by the number of things you added together.

Revisit your hypothesis. Did color matter? Which color feeder was most attractive to the birds that visited your yard? Why do you think you saw these results? Is there something you could do differently the next time you perform this experiment?

TERRIFIC TERRA COTTA BIRD BATH

IT'S EASY TO MAKE A YARD APPEALING TO BIRDS OF ALL TYPES. JUST LIKE YOU WERE ABLE TO PLANT AND MAKE A FEW THINGS TO ENCOURAGE BUTTERFLIES AND OTHER ANIMALS TO MOVE INTO YOUR YARD, YOU CAN DO THE SAME WITH BIRDS.

IT'S JUST A MATTER OF FIGURING OUT WHAT TYPES OF THINGS THEY LIKE AND NEED AND PROVIDING IT FOR THEM. BIRDS NEED A LOT OF THE SAME THINGS YOU AND I DO. THEY NEED FOOD, WATER AND A COZY PLACE TO RAISE THEIR BABIES SAFELY.

IF YOU HAVE A VARIETY OF TREES AND SHRUBS IN YOUR YARD, YOU'RE ALREADY PART OF THE WAY THERE. IF YOU HAVE FEEDERS, NESTING BOXES AND WATER SOURCES, YOUR BIRD FRIENDS WILL HELP YOU KEEP THE INSECT POPULATION UNDER CONTROL.

HERE IS A FUN AND EASY WAY TO GET STARTED ATTRACTING BIRDS TO YOUR YARD.

MATERIALS

12-inch (30-cm) terra cotta pot

14-inch (35-cm) terra cotta pot

16-inch (40-cm) terra cotta pot

18- to 20-inch (45- to 50-cm) terra cotta saucer

Silicone adhesive, epoxy or caulk

Tiles, shells, gems or other decorative items

Acrylic paint

Acrylic sealer

Your Nature Journal (page 12)

INSTRUCTIONS

You can unleash your creativity with this project and maybe even make a few bird baths as gifts for friends.

First, head outside, and turn your terra cotta pots upside down, stacking them on top of one another from largest to smallest. Secure each with the adhesive of your choice (whatever strong glue you have), but have a grown-up help you. Attach the saucer right side up tightly to the top of the stack.

Now it's time to get creative. You can glue on the tiles like a mosaic or add the gems and stones. You can also paint it. Whatever you choose to do, seal it with acrylic or another type of sealer so it's weather proof.

Fill the saucer with water and put it in a sunny spot near where birds visit regularly. Then set up somewhere discreet and observe your visitors, noting which species visit, and draw observations in your nature journal.

> **FUN FACT:** The penguin is the only bird that walks upright. It can also swim really well, but cannot fly. It uses its wings like flippers.

MAGICAL MILK CARTON HOMES FOR YOUR BIRD FRIENDS

DID YOU KNOW THAT THERE ARE SPECIFIC REQUIREMENTS DEPENDING ON THE TYPE OF BIRDS YOU WANT TO ATTRACT TO NESTING BOXES AND BIRD HOUSES IN YOUR YARD? YOU CAN MAKE SEVERAL INEXPENSIVE CUSTOM NESTING BOXES USING THE CHART BELOW TO HELP YOU WITH YOUR DIMENSIONS.

WHICH BIRD DO YOU WANT TO ATTRACT FIRST? LET'S GET STARTED!

MATERIALS

Empty, clean half-gallon (2-L) milk carton

Masking tape

Dark colored paint

Scissors

Wire

Your Nature Journal (page 12)

INSTRUCTIONS

First, bring all your materials outside to set up your crafting station. Then, take the clean half-gallon (2-L) milk carton and cover the entire thing with masking tape so that none of the carton shows through. You may need to overlap a few times.

Paint the entire carton with the dark-colored paint. We've used black, brown and have even covered nesting boxes like this with black shoe polish! Let it dry completely.

Decide what type of bird you want to attract to your yard. Check a field guide or the Internet to make sure that they are likely to be in your area before you take the time to make the box. Look at the chart to determine where your cuts need to be:

SPECIES	HEIGHT OF ENTRANCE	DIAMETER OF HOLE	HEIGHT FROM GROUND
Bluebird	6 inches (15 cm)	1½ inches (38 mm)	5 to 10 feet (1.75 to 3 m)
Chickadee	6 to 8 inches (15 to 20 cm)	1⅛ inches (28 mm)	6 to 15 feet (2 to 5 m)
Titmouse	6 to 8 inches (15 to 20 cm)	1¼ inches (31 mm)	6 to 15 feet (2 to 5 m)
Robin	8 inches (20 cm)	1 Side Open	6 to 15 feet (2 to 5 m)
Barn Swallow	6 inches (15 cm)	1 Side Open	8 to 10 feet (2.5 to 3 m)

(continued)

First, cut the entrance hole and make several small holes in the bottom of the carton to allow rainwater to drain out.

Make a few holes in the top of the carton to allow condensation to escape, too.

Finally, use the wire to hang your nesting box from a tree at the correct height for the species you chose. Make sure you hang this in the early spring so birds have time to find it and build their nests before it's time to lay eggs. Watch and wait! Your new friends will come home soon!

FUNNIES: WHAT BIRD IS WITH YOU AT EVERY MEAL?

A SWALLOW!

PINECONE FEEDERS

MAKING PINECONE FEEDERS IS ONE OF THOSE ACTIVITIES THAT IS SO SIMPLE AND FUN THAT MOST PEOPLE TRY DOING IT AT SOMETIME IN THEIR LIFE. MAKE IT A SCIENCE EXPERIMENT, THOUGH, WITH THIS SIMPLE TWIST. . . .

MATERIALS

4 large, open pinecones

Purchased bird suet or lard

Cornmeal

Rolled oats

Peanut butter

Yarn or twine

Birdseed

Dried fruit

Your Nature Journal (page 12)

INSTRUCTIONS

This can get a little messy, so head outside to make up these birdfeeders.

Mix each of the following recipes until well blended:

½ CUP (67 G) SUET WITH 2½ CUPS (426 G) CORNMEAL

½ CUP (67 G) SUET WITH 2½ CUPS (201 G) ROLLED OATS

½ CUP (90 G) PEANUT BUTTER WITH 2½ CUPS (426 G) CORNMEAL

½ CUP (90 G) PEANUT BUTTER WITH 2½ CUPS (201 G) ROLLED OATS

Tie your yarn or twine to your pinecones and cover each with a different mixture.

Roll them in birdseed and dried fruit and tap off any excess. Hang them outside in a tree for the birds. Which one do you think the birds will eat clean first? Make your prediction in your nature journal. Check back every few hours each day until the first is picked clean and record your results. Why do you think the birds preferred that choice? Was it the one you predicted they'd like best?

MORE FUN: Robins lay eggs that are pretty blue with sandy speckles on them. You can make a simple craft by painting a piece of construction paper light blue, and then sprinkling sand in the wet paint. Let it dry, then cut out an egg shape and hang it up!

MAGNIFICENT MILK CARTON BIRD FEEDER

HERE'S ANOTHER FUN THING TO DO WITH ALL OF THOSE USED MILK CARTONS YOU HAVE EACH WEEK. YOU MADE A BIRDHOUSE ON PAGE 149, NOW GIVE THOSE NEW FEATHERED RESIDENTS A PLACE TO EAT WITH A SIMPLE BIRD FEEDER.

MATERIALS

Ruler

Half gallon (2-L) milk carton, cleaned and dried

Scissors

Yarn or twine

Birdseed

Your Nature Journal (page 12)

INSTRUCTIONS

Head out to your favorite workspace in the yard with all of your materials. Using your ruler, mark a line 2½ inches (6 cm) up on two adjoining sides of the carton. Mark a line on those same two sides 2½ inches (6 cm) down. Cut the sides out along your lines so that your carton looks like the one in the picture.

Decorate your bird feeder in any way that you want to.

Punch a hole in the top of the carton and tie your yarn or twine through it and around a tree branch. Fill the feeder with birdseed. Hang out in the yard with your nature journal and wait for your new feathered friends to discover the buffet. Record the birds that come to eat.

MORE FUN: Think about what other things you can repurpose around your house to make bird feeders. Try to make some unique feeders to hang in your yard.

TASTY FRUIT AND VEGGIE FEEDERS

BIRD FEEDERS CAN BE MADE WITH JUST ABOUT ANYTHING. EVEN FRUITS AND VEGETABLES . . . ONCE YOU GATHER THE DIFFERENT SUPPLIES LISTED BELOW, YOU CAN HEAD OUTSIDE AND MAKE A BUNCH OF DIFFERENT TYPES OF FEEDERS TO HAVE OUTSIDE FOR YOUR BIRD FRIENDS TO ENJOY. CHECK IT OUT!

MATERIALS

Ears of corn—dried or fresh

Apples

Oranges

Peanut butter

Birdseed

Small cut-up pieces of fruit (apples, oranges, grapes, peaches, nectarines, etc.) and dried fruit (raisins, cranberries)

Wooden kabob skewers

Yarn or twine

Your Nature Journal (page 12)

INSTRUCTIONS

To start, bring all the materials outside to your workspace.

For the Corn: Peel the husks downward, leaving them attached. Use the yarn or twine to tie the husks together and hang them upside down in the trees.

For Apples and Oranges: Cut the fruit in half. Spread peanut butter on the peel side and roll it in birdseed. Stick a wooden skewer all the way through the fruit so it sticks out on either side. Tie yarn or twine to the skewer and hang it in a tree.

Bird Kabobs: Thread pieces of dried and fresh fruit on a wooden skewer. Tie yarn or twine to it and hang it in the trees.

Garden Garland: Tie your string or yarn to a wooden skewer and thread chunks of fresh and dried fruit onto the yarn. Tie off the ends. Drape it in shrubs and bushes.

Once you have made a few different fruit and vegetable feeders, put them out in your yard and observe. What types of birds come to eat? Do other animals like them too? Which type seems to be the most popular? Record your observations in your nature journal.

FUN FACT: An owl can turn its head almost in a complete circle, but it cannot move its eyes. Pretty cool!

RADICAL RECYCLED LOG SUET FEEDERS

SOME BIRDS LIKE WOODPECKERS AND STARLINGS PREFER EATING BIRD SUET, WHICH IS A BIRDSEED AND LARD MIXTURE. YOU CAN MAKE A SUPER AWESOME BIRD SUET FEEDER OUT OF A LOG. IT'S EASY, JUST TRY IT!

MATERIALS

Thick branch or a small log (between 4 and 8 inches [10 and 20 cm] thick)

Drill with a 1- to 1½-inch (2.5- to 4-cm) diameter bit

Large eye screw

Bird suet, homemade (page 157) or store-bought

Rope

Your Nature Journal (page 12)

INSTRUCTIONS

Have an adult help you drill several 1-inch (2.5-cm) deep holes around the log to make wells for the suet to go. Then, screw the eye screw into the top of your log feeder.

Fill in each of the holes with suet feed.

Hang your log feeder with rope from a sturdy branch on a tree outside. Which birds come to this feeder? Are they different species than those you've seen at other feeders you've made? Why do you think that is? Record your observation in your nature journal.

FUNNIES: WHAT KIND OF BIRD CAN CARRY THE MOST WEIGHT?

A CRANE!

PEANUT BUTTER SUET

CAN'T GET TO THE STORE TO BUY BIRD SUET TO FILL THE LOG FEEDER YOU MADE ON PAGE 156? TRY THIS EASY-PEASY RECIPE USING THINGS THAT ARE RIGHT INSIDE YOUR KITCHEN. YOU'LL HAVE FLOCKS OF BIRDS VISITING YOU IN NO TIME!

MATERIALS

1 cup (180 g) peanut butter

1 cup (220 g) lard

2 cups (322 g) quick cooking oats

2 cups (341 g) cornmeal

1 to 2 cups (125 to 249 g) flour

INSTRUCTIONS

Melt the lard and peanut butter in a saucepan. Add in the other ingredients, stirring in flour just until it's no longer runny. Pour it into small containers like recycled yogurt or margarine containers. Store these in the refrigerator until you're ready to use them.

You can hang this feed in mesh bags (like produce comes in), suet cages (sold at most big box stores) or stuff it into the holes in your log feeder (page 156). Observe which birds come to enjoy the suet in different containers!

STUFFED BIRD LOAF

THIS JUST MIGHT BE THE EASIEST BIRD FEEDER YOU'LL EVER MAKE!

MATERIALS

Large loaf of stale bread (set it out overnight to harden)

Peanut butter

Cornmeal

Dried fruit

Nuts

Your Nature Journal (page 12)

INSTRUCTIONS

On a table outside, cut off one end of the bread loaf and hollow it by scooping the soft insides out. You can crumble the heel and the insides and spread it out in your garden for the birds to eat. Mix peanut butter, cornmeal, fruit and nuts together and stuff the mixture inside the loaf until it's overflowing. Set the bird loaf out on a table, platform or rock pile in your garden for the birds to snack on.

Watch and see which types of birds like eating this loaf. Make observations in your nature journal.

> **FUN FACT:** Birds can eat twice their weight in food every day! So, when someone tells you they "eat like a bird," you can tell them that it doesn't really mean what they think it means, since most people say that to mean they don't eat a lot.

HAPPY HUMMINGBIRD FEEDER

HUMMINGBIRDS ARE ONE OF MY FAVORITE THINGS TO ATTRACT TO MY YARD. I JUST LOVE WATCHING THEM DART BACK AND FORTH. THEIR MOVEMENTS ARE SO COOL.

IT'S EASY TO MAKE THEM SIMPLE FEEDERS SO YOU CAN ATTRACT MORE OF THEM USING THINGS FROM AROUND YOUR HOUSE INSTEAD OF BUYING THE GLOBE FEEDERS MOST PEOPLE BUY WHEN THEY CHOOSE TO FEED HUMMINGBIRDS. THESE ARE COLORFUL AND ENTICING TO THE LITTLE SPEEDSTERS.

MATERIALS

Hammer

Nail

Clean baby food jar

Colorful plastic pieces

Hot glue gun

1 cup (192 g) sugar

4 cups (946 ml) water

Yarn or twine

Your Nature Journal (page 12)

INSTRUCTIONS

Using the hammer and nail, poke several small holes in the metal lid of the baby food jar—having an adult help you if needed. Hot glue colorful plastic petals around the holes to decorate the feeder and make it more appealing to the birds you're trying to attract. Hummingbirds seem to like bright colors, so I like to use reds, oranges and yellows.

Mix up some simple nectar by combining 1 cup (192 g) sugar and 4 cups (946 ml) water in a saucepan (with adult help) over medium heat and stirring until it comes to a boil and the sugar dissolves. Let it cool and store it in the refrigerator.

When the nectar is cool, pour it in the jar and tighten the lid securely. Tie a piece of yarn or twine on your jar and hang it near a window. Watch and see if hummingbirds find it. Watch how they sip. They'll stick their long beaks into the holes you've made and lap up the sweet nectar with their super-fast tongues. In your nature journal, keep track of how many hummingbirds start to visit once they discover you're feeding them.

FUN FACT: Hummingbirds can fly at speeds higher than 33 miles per hour (54 km per hour) and are the only birds capable of flying backwards.

FOOTPRINT ROBIN

WE LOVE DOING CRAFTS AND ART OUTSIDE WHEN THE WEATHER IS NICE—ESPECIALLY PROJECTS LIKE THIS THAT CELEBRATE THE THINGS WE'RE LEARNING ABOUT. AFTER STUDYING THE BIRDS THAT COME TO ALL OF YOUR NEW FEEDERS, YOU'LL BE ABLE TO RECOGNIZE THE MARKINGS ON THE DIFFERENT VISITORS YOU HOST. YOU COULD MAKE LOTS OF DIFFERENT PAINTINGS TO SHOW WHO'S VISITING.

MATERIALS

Heavy paper

Brown, red and orange paint

Paintbrushes

Black marker

Nature treasures like sticks, leaves and pebbles (optional)

Glue (optional)

INSTRUCTIONS

First, bring the materials to your favorite outdoor workspace. Paint the bottom of one of your bare feet completely brown. Step onto the center of a piece of art paper. Try to set your foot down evenly and firmly.

Lift your foot and clean it off while the footprint dries.

Using your red paint, add the robin's red breast. Add feet and a beak with your orange paint (or mix a little orange and brown together), and add an eye with your black marker.

That looks great, doesn't it? But, maybe you can make it look more like the robins that hang out in your own yard. Take some time to observe your feathered friends and add some of their unique markings to your painting. You could even gather some nature treasures to glue on to the background to make the painting look more realistic.

MORE FUN: What other types of footprint birds could you and your friends make? Make a flock of different bird types using a field guide for inspiration.

FUN FACT: Male birds tend to have the prettiest colors, most elaborate dances and attractive songs. Female birds choose them based on those characteristics.

BACKYARD BOTANY

(BÄT-NĒ)

FLOWERS, MOSSES, FERNS AND FUN

There are so many different plants, flowers and trees to study in your yard! Botany is the study of plants—from the smallest duckweed to the largest redwood trees. Because there is so much to cover in this field (algae, fungi, lichens, trees, ferns, flowering plants, etc.), most botanists focus in one major area of study. You'll focus on things most of you can find in your own backyard or near your home in this section.

That includes how plants work, what they look like, where they grow and how people make use of plants. Plants are essential to life. They provide food—either directly or indirectly. They also give us oxygen.

Plants also provide medicine, fibers for making clothes and other things we use to live. They're such an important part of our ecosystem, and can be found everywhere. Let's learn all about them!

CRAZY CAPILLARY ACTION

PLANT EXPERIMENT ONE

FIRST, SPILL A LITTLE BIT OF WATER INTO A TRAY ON THE TABLE. THE WATER POOLS UP BECAUSE IT IS STICKY. THE FORCES OF COHESION MAKE WATER MOLECULES STAY CLOSE TOGETHER, AND THE FORCES OF ADHESION MAKE SOME OF THOSE MOLECULES STICK TO THE TABLE TRAY.

CAPILLARY ACTION HAPPENS WHEN ADHESION IS STRONGER THAN COHESION. SO, FIRST, YOU CAN THANK COHESION FOR KEEPING THAT WATER IN A NICE NEAT PUDDLE. THEN, YOU CAN THANK THE ADHESION FORCES THAT CAUSE CAPILLARY ACTION AS YOU TAKE A PAPER TOWEL AND DIP IT INTO THE PUDDLE ON YOUR TRAY.

DO YOU SEE THE WATER CLIMBING THE FIBERS AND MOVING TO THE SPACES BETWEEN AND INSIDE OF THEM? PLANTS WOULDN'T BE ABLE TO LIVE WITHOUT CAPILLARY ACTION.

TO SEE CAPILLARY ACTION IN, WELL . . . ACTION, TRY THIS FUN ACTIVITY!

MATERIALS

4 clear glass or plastic cups or jars

Water

Food dye in four colors

Three white flowers (this is one you might want a little outside help for—you can ask an adult to buy 3 white carnations from a florist for you)

Scissors

Paper towels

Your Nature Journal (page 12)

INSTRUCTIONS

Fill each jar two-thirds full with water. Color each one differently with the food dye. Then cut the bottoms off the stems of your three carnations.

Put one flower in the jar of your choice. Then, put another flower in a second jar of your choice. Take the last flower and slit the stem of it up to about an inch (2.5 cm) from the top with scissors. The last flower should seem to have two stems now.

Put one of those stems into one of the two remaining jars and the other stem into the other jar. Place those flowers in the house in a sunny window so you can watch what happens. Over the course of the next few days, you'll see how capillary action works as the colored water moves up each stem into the flower petals. It's especially cool to see that the flower with the split stem takes on both colors.

So, what does this mean for taking care of your backyard plants? How should you water them? Since plants pull both water and nutrients from the soil, it's important to water them at their base so the water soaks into the ground by their roots.

MORE FUN: Try this with other plants. Celery in colored water is a common demonstrator of capillary action. What about other plants, though? Roses? Ferns? What else could you experiment with?

LEAF CHROMATOGRAPHY FUN
PLANT EXPERIMENT TWO

YOU MIGHT KNOW THAT LEAVES CONTAIN CHLOROPHYLL—THE CHEMICAL THAT MAKES THEM LOOK GREEN—BUT DID YOU KNOW THAT THERE ARE OTHER PIGMENTS IN THERE?

CAROTENOIDS (YELLOW AND ORANGE PIGMENTS) AND ANTHOCYANINS (RED PIGMENTS) ARE IN THERE, TOO. THE CHLOROPHYLL HANGS OUT IN THE LEAVES, DOING ITS PHOTOSYNTHESIS THING, UNTIL AUTUMN WHEN IT BEGINS TO BREAK DOWN. THE OTHER COLORS ARE LEFT FOR ALL TO SEE ONCE THAT HAPPENS.

THIS FUN ACTIVITY WILL HELP YOU FIND THE HIDDEN COLORS IN THE LEAVES AROUND YOUR YARD.

MATERIALS

Green leaves

Small glass jars

Rubbing alcohol

Plastic wrap

Hot water

A glass bowl

Tape

Coffee filters, cut into 1-inch (2.5-cm) wide strips

Pencils

Your Nature Journal (page 12)

INSTRUCTIONS

Break up the leaves you've gathered into separate jars (one leaf type per jar), and cover them with rubbing alcohol. Label the jars with the type of leaf you have in them. Cover the jars with plastic wrap so the alcohol doesn't evaporate.

Set the jars into a bowl of hot water, but don't submerge them. The alcohol will start to turn green after about a half an hour. When this happens, tape one coffee filter strip to a pencil for each jar you have. Rest a pencil on the opening of each jar so the filter strips just dip into the pigment and alcohol mixture.

Let those sit for an hour to an hour and a half.

Come back and check on the pigments. You should see that the colors began to creep up the filter strips and separate. Which type of leaf had colors that separated the most drastically? Which had bright pigments? Which were more subdued? What color do you think each tree's leaves will become in the fall? Write your observations in your nature journal.

FUN FACT: It is estimated that there are about 50,000 edible plant species in the world, but that most humans only eat about 20 of them. Think about all of the foods you are missing out on!

PHOTOSYNTHESIS ACTION
PLANT EXPERIMENT THREE

PHOTOSYNTHESIS HAPPENS WHEN A PLANT HARNESSES THE ENERGY FROM THE SUN TO PRODUCE FOOD. CHLOROPHYLLS ARE FOUND IN THE LEAF AND ABSORB THE ENERGY FROM THE SUNLIGHT. THIS ENERGY SPLITS WATER MOLECULES IN THE PLANT INTO HYDROGEN AND OXYGEN.

THE OXYGEN IS RELEASED THROUGH THE PLANT'S LEAVES INTO THE ATMOSPHERE. THE LEFTOVER HYDROGEN MIXES WITH CARBON DIOXIDE THAT COMES IN THROUGH SMALL PORES, CALLED STOMATA, IN THE PLANT'S LEAVES AND MAKES GLUCOSE. SOME OF THAT GLUCOSE GIVES IMMEDIATE ENERGY TO THE PLANT FOR GROWTH AND DEVELOPMENT. SOME IS STORED IN THE FRUIT, LEAVES AND ROOTS FOR THE PLANT TO USE LATER.

THIS IS A SIMPLE DEMONSTRATION OF WHAT HAPPENS WHEN LIGHT CAN'T REACH THE LEAVES OF A PLANT TO TRIGGER THE PROCESS OF PHOTOSYNTHESIS IN YOUR OWN BACKYARD.

MATERIALS

Two identical plants with large leaves

Heavy cardstock

Paper clips

Your Nature Journal (page 12)

INSTRUCTIONS

Explore in your backyard to find two identical plants that have large leaves. You can plant them if you don't have any—just have your parents help you get some inexpensive potted plants at the garden center. You can also do this activity on a house plant. It won't do any long-term damage to your plant.

Make sure that both plants are in an equally sunny location. Clip heavy cardstock on several of the large leaves of one of the plants. The second plant will be your control plant. What do you think will happen if you leave the plant's leaves covered for a week? Make a hypothesis in your nature journal.

Gently uncover the leaves after a week of sunny days. What do you notice? Without the energy from sunlight, the plant was not able to photosynthesize and the plant's leaves have probably begun to change color and die. Write down your results in your journal. Was your hypothesis correct?

FUNNIES: WHY WAS THE PHOTOGRAPHER GREAT AT BOTANY?

SHE KNEW ALL ABOUT PHOTOSYNTHESIS!

BEAUTIFUL NATURE PATTERNS

ALTHOUGH NATURE OFTEN APPEARS TO BE RANDOM, THERE ARE ACTUALLY PATTERNS EVERYWHERE. IN FACT, THERE IS A LOT OF MATH FOUND IN NATURE! CAN YOU BELIEVE THAT? IT'S TRUE!

FOR EXAMPLE, THE FIBONACCI NUMBER PATTERN OCCURS SO OFTEN THAT SOME SCIENTISTS CONSIDER IT A BASIC LAW OF NATURE. THE FIBONACCI SEQUENCE IS A SERIES OF NUMBERS IN WHICH EACH NEW NUMBER IS THE SUM OF THE TWO NUMBERS BEFORE IT. 0, 1, 1, 2, 3, 5, 8, 13. . . .

YOU CAN SEE THE FIBONACCI SEQUENCE IN FLOWERS, SHELLS, PLANTS, LEAVES AND SO MUCH MORE. IF YOU COUNT THE SPIRAL PATTERN YOU SEE IN FLOWER PETALS, YOU'LL NOTICE THAT THE NUMBER OF PETALS IS USUALLY A NUMBER FROM THE FIBONACCI SEQUENCE. THE SAME THING CAN ALSO BE FOUND IN SEED ARRANGEMENTS ON FLOWER HEADS. GO CHECK IT OUT IN YOUR YARD!

MATERIALS

Your Nature Journal (page 12)

Camera

Nature materials (sticks, rocks, shells, etc.)

INSTRUCTIONS

Head outside and observe carefully. What examples of growing patterns can you see in your yard? Draw some of what you see in your journal. Or, you can take photos of nature patterns and tape them into your journal.

When you feel inspired, try creating a Fibonacci sequence or another pattern using natural materials. This is often called land art. Find an open area, and build a pattern with rocks, sticks, flower petals and anything else you can find.

FUNNIES: WHY WAS THE TOMATO TURNING RED?

BECAUSE IT SAW THE SALAD DRESSING!

WHY SHOULD YOU NEVER TELL A SECRET ON THE FARM?

BECAUSE THE POTATOES HAVE EYES AND THE CORN IS ALL EARS!

GROOVY CD CASE BEAN PLANT

HAVE YOU EVER PLANTED SEEDS BEFORE? THIS IS A FUN WAY TO PLANT, WATCH THE GROWTH CYCLE OF A BEAN PLANT UNFOLD AND IDENTIFY THE PARTS OF A PLANT. PLUS, IT'S EASY TO PLANT YOUR SEEDLINGS IN A SUNNY PLACE IN YOUR YARD ONCE YOU'RE DONE OBSERVING IT IN ITS CASE.

MATERIALS

Empty CD cases

Soil

Variety of vegetable seeds (try to have at least one lima bean as they grow well in this setting and you can really see the parts of a plant when looking at a bean seedling)

Permanent marker

Droppers

Your Nature Journal (page 12)

INSTRUCTIONS

Do this activity outside so you can enjoy nature and don't make a mess in the house. Open up the CD cases and make sure the hinges are at the top. Put about an inch and a half (3 cm) of soil in the bottom. Plant one seed in each of your CD cases. Close the cases and label them with the permanent marker so you know what type of plant is in each. Stand your CD garden in a bright sunny window, watering each case every day by dripping water with a medicine dropper at the hinge on the top.

In your nature journal, draw what you see every few days to help in your observations of a plant's growing cycle. Remember that roots pull water and nutrients up from the soil. Do you see them growing downward and spreading through the soil to search for nutrients?

Remember that leaves need to pull energy from sunlight to make food for the plant. Do you see the leaves reaching upward towards the sunlight? Once your plants have started growing nice big leaves to replace the baby leaves, called cotyledon, that first sprout from the seed, you'll know that it's time to transplant your garden outside. You can grow these seedlings in a garden or in large containers.

MORE FUN: What else could you grow your seedlings in? My kids had fun growing five different types of seeds in the fingers of a plastic glove that they had hung on the window this year. You could try that or grow it in something else.

FANTASTIC FLOWER DISSECTION

THIS IS A COOL WAY TO SEE ALL OF THE DIFFERENT PARTS OF THE INSIDE OF A FLOWER, BUT YOU NEED TO ASK AN ADULT FOR PERMISSION TO USE THE CRAFT KNIFE OR HAVE THEM MAKE THE CUTS FOR YOU. BE SAFE, AND YOU'LL BE ABLE TO DISCOVER LOTS OF AMAZING THINGS AS YOU EXPLORE THE INSIDES OF THE FLOWERS IN YOUR YARD!

MATERIALS

Several flowers with big blooms

Tray or white piece of paper

Craft knife

Your Nature Journal (page 12)

INSTRUCTIONS

Bring the materials to your favorite workspace in your yard. Set one flower on a tray or a white piece of paper to make it easy to see all of the parts. (You have several flowers just in case you make a bad cut on one. Just put the extras in water and enjoy them as a decoration until you need them.)

First, take a minute to identify the flower, stem and leaves of your flower. These are the outside parts of the flower that most people pay attention to. Once you've identified those, it's time to check out the inside of your bloom.

Take your craft knife (with adult supervision), and gently press it into the petals, pulling it through the top layer of petals, the base of the flower and all the way down the stem. Be careful not to cut all the way through—you'll want to be able to open the flower up and lay it flat to look inside.

Begin at the top of the flower. Gently pull the petals apart on either side of your cut. First, you'll see the male parts of the flower. Those are called the stamen, and are the long tubes that have the powdery pollen on their tips. The tips with the pollen are called anthers.

When you keep pulling apart the petals and separating the stamen, you'll find one long tube in the middle. This is the female part of the flower and is called the pistil. The pistil is usually taller than the stamen and has a sticky tip called the stigma.

Look at those parts closely. For a flower to be pollinated and reproduce, pollen from the anthers of one flower needs to be transferred to the stigma of another flower. Bees are great pollinators. They get pollen on their feet when they visit one flower, and it rubs off on another flower when they switch.

If you take a look at the base of the flower where the stamen and pistil come together, you'll see a bulge. This is another female part, called the ovary. Slit that open really carefully. There are little ovules in there—small eggs. When a plant is pollinated, fertilization takes place and those eggs will develop into seeds. Pretty cool, isn't it?

FUN FACT: Some plants are carnivorous, which means that they get their nutrients by eating small insects and spiders. The Venus flytrap is one of my favorites.

COOL GARDENS YOU CAN GROW

THE BEST WAY TO LEARN ABOUT PLANTS IS TO GROW THEM. And, one of the most interesting ways to garden is to create a themed garden or two. We have a lot of fun with this every year, and have grown all sorts of gardens over the years. I'm sharing some of our family's favorite garden types here.

Pick whichever you like, try a new one each year or grow a few different kinds . . . just get out and grow something! It's a lot of fun.

PIZZA GARDEN

DO YOU LIKE HOMEMADE PIZZA? WE LOVE IT HERE AT OUR HOUSE. HERE'S A FUN WAY TO GROW YOUR OWN PIZZA DURING THE SUMMER—AND A FUN RECIPE TO USE THE INGREDIENTS ONCE THEY'RE MATURE. COOKING IS SCIENCE, TOO!

MATERIALS

Seeds (or seedlings) for pizza ingredients: basil, oregano, parsley, onions, tomatoes, peppers

A circular place in the yard for a garden OR a large pot for a container garden

Soil

Your Nature Journal (page 12)

INSTRUCTIONS

Decide if you're going to plant a large container garden or one in the ground. If you are planting a container garden, get your pot ready by filling it with soil. Divide your container or plot of land into six wedges like pizza slices. Plant your seeds or seedlings—one type of plant per "slice."

Label your garden sections. We like to use craft sticks that we decorate with permanent markers.

Make sure your garden is in a sunny spot, and water it every day. There's so much science involved in growing gardens like this. How much water is not enough? How much is too much? Are the plants getting enough sunlight? How quickly are they growing? You can make all of these observations and answer all of these questions in your journal as you take care of your pizza garden.

When it's ready to harvest, you'll just need an adult to help you make the pizza sauce using your garden ingredients and buy a store bought pizza crust and cheese. Yum!

MORE FUN:

PIZZA GARDEN PIZZA RECIPE

INGREDIENTS

6-8 tomatoes

1 clove garlic, minced

2 tbsp (5 g) chopped basil

2 tbsp (5 g) chopped oregano

1 tbsp (2.5 g) thyme

2 tbsp (5 g) parsley

1 tsp salt

½ tsp pepper

Prepared pizza crust

Mozarella cheese

Chopped peppers

INSTRUCTIONS

Put the tomatoes in a pot of boiling water for 30 seconds, and then put them into a bowl of ice water. Use a paring knife to remove the tomato skins once they've cooled down. Cut out the core and seeds of the tomatoes and dice them up.

Bring your tomatoes, garlic, herbs, salt and pepper to a simmer in a pot over medium heat for 30 minutes. Spread the sauce on a prepared pizza crust, sprinkle lots of cheese and chopped peppers on top. Bake it in a 350°F (177°C) oven until the cheese is warm and bubbly. Yum! Enjoy!

MAGICAL FAIRY GARDEN

WE MAKE FAIRY GARDENS EVERY SINGLE SUMMER. EACH YEAR LOOKS DIFFERENT THAN THE YEAR BEFORE,
BUT EACH ONE IS JUST AS GREAT AS THE LAST ONE. THEY KEY TO A BEAUTIFUL AND FUN FAIRY GARDEN IS THAT
IT'S MEANT TO BE INTERACTED WITH AND PLAYED IN.

MATERIALS

Brightly colored flowers and small plants

Fairy houses (store-bought or handmade)

Pretty stones, gems, shells and other fun things to decorate with

A large container or small area of the yard

Soil

Your Nature Journal (page 12)

INSTRUCTIONS

For our fairy garden, we blocked off a small plot of ground near our garage. There's a brick wall and brightly colored flowers planted in a rainbow pattern—this has been named Rainbow Woods. Behind Rainbow Woods is a rock structure my kids built.

Coming out of Rainbow Woods, fairies (or the dollhouse people my kids play with in the garden) can follow a path made out of shells that leads to Fairy Village. The village is made up of birdhouses we found at a garage sale and one fairy house made out of an unfinished wooden birdhouse with a bark and stick ladder. Surrounding the homes are gardens full of plastic and glass gems (because fairies like shiny objects) and more small plants.

Fairy gardens are fun because you can plant whatever you have on hand, and use old toys, logs, rocks, sticks and other scraps to make homes and play structures out of. They important thing is to have fun with nature and your imagination.

You can hang out and see the new critters that come to join the fairies in their garden. Tiny tree frogs, worms and insects might make their homes there, too. It's fun to sketch the changes in your nature journal as the garden grows throughout the summer.

MORE FUN: Fairy Lore

- Fairies range in size from tinier than a firefly to bigger than a giant.

- Laughter and imagination attracts them.

- A ripple in the air or water, or a sudden chill indicates they're there.

- They love music, bells and rhymes, and they love to dance.

- If you're missing small objects, there might be fairies around.

- Their favorite things to eat are milk, honey and nectar.

JUICE POUCH GARDEN

WANT TO ADD A LITTLE FUN AND WHIMSY TO YOUR YARD? TRY THIS SIMPLE GARDEN IDEA WITH SOME OF THOSE JUICE POUCHES LEFT OVER FROM LUNCHES OR TRIPS TO THE ZOO.

MATERIALS

Empty juice pouches

Scissors

Soil

Several types of garden seeds

Craft sticks

Permanent markers

Your Nature Journal (page 12)

INSTRUCTIONS

Cut off the tops of the pouches and clean them out really well. Poke a few holes in the bottom so water can drain out. Fill them up with soil and plant a few seeds in each by poking a hole in the soil with your finger, dropping the seeds in and covering them with soil. Make sure each pouch has a different type of seed.

Label each pouch with the type of seed you planted with a decorated craft stick and the permanent marker.

Make a prediction in your journal. Which type of seed do you think will grow the quickest? Why? Every day, water the pouches a little and draw what you observe in your nature journal. Even if you don't see any changes, draw that. You'll use those observations to come to conclusions about how quickly plants grow and can use that information in the future when you plant again next spring.

> **MORE FUN:** Try these other fun garden ideas, too!
>
> ❁ Shoe Garden—Plant flowers in old shoes. This is fun and quirky and adds whimsy to a fairy or container garden in your yard.
>
> ❁ Edible Flower Garden—Chose edible flowers like lavender, thyme, chives, nasturtiums, daylily, dill or basil and plant those in a garden to eat in a salad.
>
> ❁ Purse Garden—Line old bags and purses with plastic bags and plant flowers and herbs in them. You can hang those from a fence in the yard for a fun backyard garden.

BACKYARD ECOLOGY
(Ē'KÄLEJĒ)
HOW IT ALL COMES TOGETHER

Ecology is the study of the relationships between living organisms and their environment. It's how we understand the connections between us, the plants, reptiles, insects and anything else in our backyards. It includes how those living things interact with each other and their own physical environment—the climate, water, soil and more.

Ecologists tend to specialize in a specific type of ecosystem—and you are going to be an ecologist that studies your own backyard ecosystem!

MYSTERIES FOUND IN A SQUARE YARD: YOUR ECOLOGICAL SURVEY SITE

HERE'S A CHANCE FOR YOU TO DO A LITTLE ECOLOGICAL FIELD WORK IN YOUR OWN BACKYARD. RANDOM SAMPLING IS WHEN ECOLOGISTS MAKE AN ESTIMATE OF THE POPULATIONS OF DIFFERENT SPECIES IN AN AREA BY CALCULATING WHAT THEY SEE IN A SMALL SECTION.

IT CAN BE REALLY INTERESTING TO SEE THE BIODIVERSITY, OR VARIETY OF LIFE, THAT IS LIVING RIGHT IN YOUR OWN GRASSY BACKYARD. YOU'RE GOING TO SECTION OFF A SQUARE YARD (SQUARE METER) OF LAND IN YOUR BACKYARD WHERE YOU CAN DO SOME OF THE EXPERIMENTS IN THIS CHAPTER. A YARD IS THE SAME AS THREE FEET (1 M), AND A SQUARE YARD IS A SQUARE SECTION WITH FOUR EQUAL YARD-LENGTH (METER) SIDES.

MATERIALS

Tape measure

Wooden stakes or sticks

Twine or string

Your Nature Journal (page 12)

INSTRUCTIONS

Measure a square yard (square meter) of land, and mark each corner with a wooden stake or stick in the ground. Wrap twine or string around the stakes, creating an enclosure. This is your ecological survey site.

The first thing you'll do, once you set up your site, is to sit quietly with your nature journal and observe. Then, after you've sat awhile, write down any initial observations you have about the site. Draw it, adding in as many details as you can. Scientists need to know what normally happens in observation sites so that they know when there is a problem. You're observing to figure out what usually happens in your yard when you're able to sit quietly.

> **MORE FUN:** Use a piece of paper or cardboard and make a sign so others know not to disturb your scientific test site. Our sign reads, "This is an ecological survey site. Please do not disturb the area or any equipment." You can staple it to the twine wrapped around the stakes, or attach it to another stake and put it in the ground next to your survey site.

ANIMAL POPULATIONS IN YOUR ECOLOGICAL SURVEY SITE

ECOLOGISTS NEED TO KNOW THE DISTRIBUTION OF ANIMALS IN THE ECOSYSTEM THEY ARE STUDYING. THIS HELPS THEM DISCOVER THE BIOLOGICAL AND PHYSICAL FACTORS THAT ARE IMPORTANT TO AN ANIMAL'S SURVIVAL. THEY CAN COMPARE THIS INFORMATION TO HISTORICAL DATA FOR THE AREA.

WHEN SCIENTISTS STUDY AREAS AND THEIR DATA OVER TIME, THEY CAN IDENTIFY PATTERNS AND SEE HOW POPULATIONS MIGHT BE CHANGING IN THE FUTURE. THIS IS GREAT INFORMATION THAT CAN HELP THEM POTENTIALLY SAVE ENDANGERED SPECIES IN THE FUTURE.

WHILE YOU DON'T HAVE ENOUGH DATA TO IDENTIFY AND PROTECT ENDANGERED SPECIES IN YOUR BACKYARD, YOU CAN GET SOME PRETTY GOOD INFORMATION ABOUT WHAT IS LIVING THERE. HEAD OUT TO YOUR ECOLOGICAL SITE TO WATCH AND LEARN!

MATERIALS

Ecological Survey Site (page 182)

Magnifying glass

Your Nature Journal (page 12)

Watercolor pencils (optional)

INSTRUCTIONS

Choose a time when you won't be bothered and head outside to your backyard. Make a checklist in your nature journal with the following categories: mammals, reptiles, amphibians, insects and birds.

Find a quiet spot near your Ecological Survey Site and watch. Make a tally mark on your checklist every time you see an animal in each category. Since it sometimes takes a long period of silence and calm for animals like squirrels or rabbits—if they're around your yard—to come back, try to stay quietly observing for as long as possible. An hour is great.

You can try your hand at some nature journaling during this time. I like to use watercolor pencils and sketch the animals I see. You can do this around your checklist.

After awhile—as long as you can handle—waiting for the bigger animals to stop by, use your magnifying glass to look down into the grass in your survey site. Mark all of the insects you see.

What species surprised you? Was there anything you expected to see, but didn't? Write the answers to these questions in your nature journal, too.

MORE FUN: Try visiting your site at different times of the day. Do you see different animals at different times? Why do you suppose that is?

PLANT POPULATIONS IN YOUR ECOLOGICAL SURVEY SITE

JUST LIKE ECOLOGISTS NEED TO KNOW THE DIFFERENT ANIMALS IN A GIVEN AREA, THEY NEED TO KNOW ABOUT THE PLANT LIFE FOUND THERE, TOO. WHEN YOU GO OUT TO YOUR ECOLOGICAL SURVEY SITE THIS TIME, ARM YOURSELF WITH FIELD GUIDES TO HELP YOU IDENTIFY THE PLANTS YOU SEE. IF YOU DON'T HAVE TIME TO GO TO A LIBRARY, JUST TAKE GOOD NOTES OR CUT A LEAF FROM EACH PLANT YOU SEE TO PRESS INTO YOUR NATURE JOURNAL TO LOOK UP LATER.

MATERIALS

Ecological Survey Site (page 182)

Magnifying glass

Watercolor pencils (optional)

Plant and wildflower field guides

Your Nature Journal (page 12)

INSTRUCTIONS

Go over the entire Ecological Survey Area carefully and take note of every different type of plant you see. Draw them in your nature journal. My kids love using watercolor pencils so they can use brushes and water to blend the colors later.

Were there any types of plants that looked unfamiliar? Did you find anything cool or unusual? My son found a four-leaf clover the last time we did this. Lucky kid!!

> MORE FUN: You can preserve your plant leaves by pressing them into the pages of your nature journal. Arrange them on a page how you'd like, and close the journal. Put the journal underneath stacks of heavy books and leave it alone for a week or more. When you open it back up, you can glue your pressed leaves onto the page where you arranged them so you have them forever.

SUPER SOIL QUALITY TESTS

Soil is a mixture of minerals, water, air and both dead and alive organic matter. It's truly amazing because it makes plants grow, allows gas exchanges to happen between the land and the air, and provides the foundation of the habitats of most of the world's animals. It holds water. It cleans water. And it recycles nutrients so they keep sustaining generations of living organisms.

Keeping the soil in your yard healthy is important because it actually helps to improve the quality of everything around your backyard ecosystem. It becomes a much healthier place for you and your family to live.

AND WE ALL WANT A HEALTHY PLACE TO LIVE, RIGHT?

Soil quality is how well your soil is able to function for the way it's supposed to be used in your local ecosystem. Using the next few experiments, you can find out how healthy your soil is in your backyard. It's important to evaluate the physical, chemical and biological features in your soil sample.

FUN FACT: One shovelful of soil can contain more organisms than species in the Amazon Rainforest. Can you even believe that?! There are some teeny tiny things living in our world!

TEXTURE TEST PART ONE

SOIL EXPERIMENT ONE

THIS FIRST SOIL EXPERIMENT WILL HELP YOU DETERMINE THE PHYSICAL MAKEUP OF YOUR SOIL.

MATERIALS

Ecological Survey Site (page 182)

Shovel

Glass jar with a lid

Water

Your Nature Journal (page 12)

INSTRUCTIONS

Go out into your yard and dig up a small sample of soil from your Ecological Survey Site. (Make sure this is okay with your parents first.) Fill your jar one third full with your soil sample. Add water until the jar is about two thirds full and put the lid on tightly.

Shake the jar as hard as you can (but don't let go—that would be a mess!) and then let it settle somewhere on a shelf overnight. We have a shelf near our garden outside that my kids leave experiments like this on.

The next day, draw what your soil sample looks like in your nature journal. The coarse sand in your sample should have settled first, followed by the silt and then the clay. Can you see the layers?

Sand is the looser, more granular part of your sample. Silt is the superfine clay and sand pieces that settle as sediment. Clay is the densest part of the soil sample.

FUN FACT: One cupful of soil can contain over six billion bacteria!

TEXTURE TEST PART TWO
SOIL EXPERIMENT TWO

THIS TEST WILL TELL YOU HOW HEAVY THE CLAY CONTENT IS IN YOUR SOIL. HEAVY CLAY MEANS THE SOIL WON'T DRAIN WELL. IF THE WATER DOESN'T DRAIN OUT OF THE SOIL, THEN PLANTS WILL GET TOO MUCH WATER AND DIE.

MATERIALS

Soil sample from your Ecological Survey Site (page 182)

Water

Your Nature Journal (page 12)

INSTRUCTIONS

Moisten a small handful of soil. Squeeze it as hard as you can, then open your hand, set it down and draw what it looks like in your nature journal. Though . . . you might want to rinse and dry your hands first.

If your soil sample holds together, forming a cast, then it has a high percentage of clay in it. Write down your observations in your nature journal.

> **FUN FACT:** It can take over 1,000 years for healthy topsoil to form on its own.

HUMUS TEST
SOIL EXPERIMENT THREE

THIS TEST WILL GIVE YOU INFORMATION ON HOW WELL THE SOIL WILL GROW PLANTS. RICH HUMUS IS BETTER FOR GROWING THAN WEAK HUMUS. IT'S MORE NUTRITIOUS FOR YOUR PLANTS.

MATERIALS

Shovel

Ecological Survey Site (page 182)

Your Nature Journal (page 12)

INSTRUCTIONS

Use your shovel to take a one-foot deep by a few inches wide (30 cm deep by 6 cm wide) sample of soil from your Ecological Survey Site, and look closely at its color. Humus is the nutrient-rich organic component of soil. It's the part where decomposed leaves, worms and microorganisms are found. If your soil sample is dark—the darker the better—then it's rich in humus and is a great place to grow a garden.

Write and draw your observations in your nature journal. What did the humus content look like? Rich or weak? Would your ecological site be a nutrient-rich place for plants to grow?

CHEMISTRY TEST (PH)
SOIL EXPERIMENT FOUR

DEPENDING ON THE MAKEUP OF SOIL CHEMISTRY, FARMERS AND GARDENERS CONSIDER WHICH NUTRIENTS TO ADD IN AND WHICH PLANTS TO GROW. YOU CAN TEST THE SOIL CHEMISTRY OF YOUR ECOLOGICAL SITE WITH THIS SIMPLE ACTIVITY.

MATERIALS

Soil sample from your Ecological Survey Site (page 182)

Water

pH test strips OR baking soda and vinegar

Glass jars with lids

Your Nature Journal (page 12)

INSTRUCTIONS

Knowing the chemistry makeup of your soil can help you make good choices when you are trying to figure out what to plant. Ideally, you want your soil to have a pH reading of around seven because that's neutral and just about anything can grow.

And, while pH test strips make it super easy to test the alkalinity, or how acidic the soil is, you don't have to have them to figure out what your soil is like. If you want to be official, you can order pH strips inexpensively online or even find them at the drugstore.

If you do get pH strips, mix equal parts water and soil in your jar, put the lid on, and shake it well. Dip your test strip into the water and record your results in your nature journal. Your paper will change colors, and you should compare the color to the chart that comes with your strips. That will tell you the pH level of your sample.

WHAT DO THE PH RESULTS MEAN?

PH READING	MEANING
< 5.6	Strongly Acidic
5.6—6.2	Moderately Acidic
6.2—6.7	Slightly Acidic
6.7—7.3	Neutral
7.3—7.9	Slightly Alkaline
7.9—8.5	Moderately Alkaline
> 8.5	Strongly Alkaline

(continued)

You can find out the chemistry of your soil sample with things found around your house, too. Put 2 tablespoons (11 g) of soil each in separate jars. In the first jar, add ½ cup (118 ml) of vinegar. If it fizzes, your soil is alkaline with a pH somewhere between seven and eight.

If it doesn't fizz with the vinegar, then add water to the other jar to make the 2 tablespoons (11 g) of soil slightly muddy. Add ½ cup (102 g) baking soda to the mud. If that fizzes, then you have acidic soil, probably between pH level five and six.

If your soil didn't react at all, then it's neutral and you're super lucky! You can plant just about anything! We love trying those fizzy mud experiments. If that was fun for you, you might want to test soil samples from different areas.

Record the results of your chemistry test in your nature journal so that you have the details of the alkalinity along with the results of the other tests you've been conducting.

FUN FACT: Groundwater is water that fills in the cracks and holes in the soil. It's a huge source of freshwater for our planet, and is stored in groundwater reservoirs.

EARTHWORM TEST
SOIL EXPERIMENT FIVE

WHEN THERE ARE A LOT OF WORMS IN YOUR SOIL SAMPLE, YOU'LL KNOW THAT THE SOIL IS HEALTHY.
CHECK OUT YOUR ECOLOGICAL SITE AND FIND OUT HOW HEALTHY IT IS!

MATERIALS

Shovel

Ecological Survey Site (page 182)

Old sheet or another drop cloth

Your Nature Journal (page 12)

INSTRUCTIONS

Dig up a large square (one square foot [30 cm], if you're able to) in your Ecological Survey Site. Try to dig at least 6 inches (15 cm) down.

Spread your soil sample on your cloth. Record the measurements of the sample you dug up in your nature journal—make sure to record the width and depth.

Sift through the soil, carefully removing and counting the earthworms and other creatures you find. Earthworms are very important for the health of your soil, so the more there are, the better your soil is for growing.

FUN FACT: Worm tea is the liquid that collects in the bottom of the worm bin you made on page 85 in the Putting Worms to Work activity. You can dilute it with water and spray it on your lawn or house plants. Try it and watch them grow!

FUN FACT: An acre of healthy farmland will likely have over one million earthworms in it.

BREATHE RIGHT: KNOW THE QUALITY OF THE AIR

AIR POLLUTION HAS BEEN AROUND IN SOME FORM OR ANOTHER SINCE THE FIRST HUMANS BUILT FIRES. SMOKE FROM THOSE FIRES ROSE UP IN A HAZE AND BLOCKED THE VIEW. IT WASN'T A PROBLEM THEN. AS TIME WENT ON, AIR POLLUTION REACHED HIGH LEVELS. DURING THE INDUSTRIAL REVOLUTION, THICK SMOKE AND SOOT FROM FACTORIES CLUNG TO BUILDINGS AND HUNG IN THE AIR OF MAJOR CITIES. PEOPLE CLUED IN TO THE HEALTH ISSUES CAUSED BY THIS TYPE OF POLLUTION. SINCE THEN PEOPLE HAVE BEEN TRYING TO REDUCE THE POLLUTION IN THE AIR.

YOU CAN FIND OUT WHICH AREAS IN YOUR YARD AND NEIGHBORHOOD HAVE THE HIGHEST CONCENTRATION OF PARTICLE AIR POLLUTANTS WITH THIS SIMPLE ACTIVITY. IT'S A BIT MORE CHALLENGING TO TEST FOR CHEMICAL POLLUTANTS, BUT THIS IS A GOOD START.

MATERIALS

5 × 7 inch (13 × 18 cm) index cards or cardstock

Transparent tape

Black marker

Magnifying glass

Microscope (optional)

Your Nature Journal (page 12)

INSTRUCTIONS

Take your materials and head outside to your favorite workspace. Cut a one-inch (2.5 cm) square out of the center of two index cards. Cover the opening with tape, so that on one side of the index card, the sticky part is exposed, and choose two spots in your yard in which to place your cards.

Write the name of location #1 on one card next to the opening with the marker. Do the same thing with the other card for location #2. Tape your cards to a play structure, building, post or something else stationary in the locations you have chosen.

Make sure the sticky side of the tape faces out. Take them down after an hour and observe the particle matter stuck on each sticky square with a magnifying glass or microscope.

In your nature journal, write down what you found. What do the particles look like? Which area had more particles in the air? Was there anything that surprised you about these results?

What could you do to clean up the air in those locations? Anything? Maybe you could plant a garden to get more oxygen in that area. Or, could you put up a fence to block things from blowing into your hard? See what ideas you come up with, then go for it!

FUN FACT: People cause much of the problems we have with air pollution with things like factories, cars, airplanes, chemicals, methane from landfills and so much more. Poor air quality causes illness and environmental damage.

NASTY DETERIORATION: FIND OUT WHAT ACID RAIN DOES

AIR POLLUTANTS CAN CAUSE RAINWATER TO BECOME POLLUTED WITH CHEMICALS THAT CAN CAUSE FURTHER PROBLEMS. WE CALL POLLUTED WATER ACID RAIN. ACID RAIN IS DANGEROUS BECAUSE THE POLLUTANTS IN THE RAINWATER CAN RUIN FRESHWATER, AND DAMAGE CROPS AND FOOD SOURCES.

THE EROSION, OR WEARING DOWN, OF LIMESTONE AND MARBLE CAN RESULT IN LOST ARTWORK LIKE STATUES AND MONUMENTS THAT CAN'T BE REPLACED. ECOSYSTEMS LIKE LAKES AND RIVERS CAN BE DESTROYED WHEN THEY BECOME TOO ACIDIC, KILLING BIRDS, FISH AND PLANTS. SEE THE EFFECTS OF AN ACID ON A SUBSTANCE FOR YOURSELF.

MATERIALS

Sidewalk chalk

½ cup (118 ml) vinegar

Glass jar

Your Nature Journal (page 12)

INSTRUCTIONS

Crush up a few pieces of sidewalk chalk. Pour ½ cup (118 ml) of vinegar in the jar and add a tablespoon (8 g) of the crushed chalk. What's happening? Record your observations in your nature journal.

The chalk is made up of calcium carbonate, and it reacts when it comes into contact with an acid like vinegar. Keep adding chalk until the reaction stops. By adding more calcium carbonate, you've neutralized the reaction, using up all of the acid from the vinegar.

One of the reasons water is so clean and fresh in mountain streams is because limestone and other minerals that make up the rocks lining them neutralize the acids in rainwater before they can fill the streams!

FUN FACT: Acid rain is made when gasses get into the air. The wind blows these gasses for miles. Then, they get washed out of the air when it rains.

CITIZEN SCIENCE AT HOME

(SIDIZEN SIENS)

WHAT CAN YOU DO?

Citizen scientists are volunteers who take time to assist scientists in their research. They can support scientists by submitting data for organized projects, sharing observations or speaking out about issues. It helps scientists to have other people to help them and gives them lots of data to sift through.

There are lots of citizen science programs to choose from. You could work locally with your park systems or universities. Some of the most popular programs are national and have websites where you can study to learn specific protocols for working on their projects. Then, you can head into the field and submit your findings online.

You can find out about some popular and well-established programs in this section.

THE GREAT BACKYARD BIRD COUNT

Sponsored by the Cornell Lab of Ornithology, the Audubon Society, and Bird Studies Canada, the Great Backyard Bird Count is a yearly event that has been happening since 1998. It was the first project of its kind to collect bird data from citizen scientists, and report them in real time.

It's easy to participate. Go to gbbc.birdcount.org to register. During the count, go outside anywhere, at any time during the dates, and tally the number and types of birds you see for a minimum of 15 minutes at a time. Go online, login and report your findings. More than 160,000 people from all over the world participate in the four-day event every February.

JOURNEY NORTH

Journey North is one of the best known citizen science projects for kids. It is a global study of wildlife migration and seasonal change. It's simple to participate.

Using your nature journal, get together with a group of friends and track the migration patterns of monarch butterflies, robins, hummingbirds, whooping cranes, gray whales and other specific birds and mammals. You can also track the budding of certain plants, changing sunlight and other natural events.

The website, www.learner.org/jnorth, is full of links to reporting forms, lesson plans, activities and fun facts that help you make connections between what you're seeing and what's happening in the rest of the world.

BUGS IN OUR BACKYARD

Bugs in Our Backyard (or BioB) is a project from Colby College, and is funded by the National Science Foundation, that encourages kids to get outside and do biological surveys in their own backyards. And, hey! You already have a great Ecological Survey Site marked off in your yard from page 182. That would be the perfect place for you to sit and make observations.

You'll help scientists answer questions like: Do insects on specific plants crowd each other out? How do wing variations affect the distribution of specific insects? How does insect distribution vary over time?

You can learn more, and enter your data, on their website, www.bugsinourbackyard.org.

FROGWATCH USA

A citizen science program organized by the Association of Zoos and Aquariums, FrogWatch USA provides kids and families the chance to learn about the wetlands in their communities. They learn and document the calls of local frogs and toads during evenings from February through August, and report their data online at www.aza.org/FrogWatch.

The data that families collect helps scientists learn more so they can develop strategies for protecting these important species.

MONARCH WATCH

Monarch watch was founded in 1992 by Professor "Chip" Taylor of the University of Kansas Department of Ecology and Evolutionary Biology. Since then, thousands of volunteers from around the world have helped tag monarch butterflies in an attempt to track and understand their amazing migration.

You can find ways to participate on their website, www.monarchwatch.org, and even order milkweed seeds and plants to grow your own monarch waystation so traveling butterflies can stop and refuel in your yard along the way.

FIREFLY WATCH

Join volunteers from around the country to observe and document fireflies in your yard this summer for Firefly Watch, a project between the Museum of Science in Boston and researchers from Tufts University and Fitchburg State College. Their goal is to track fireflies and learn about their geographic distribution and activity during the summer months. You can sign up at https://legacy.mos.org/fireflywatch.

MORE RESOURCES FOR BACKYARD EXPLORATION

There are so many cool things to do with the nature you find in your own backyard! I love using all sorts of things to discover—books, tools, toys, kits and more. I've pulled together a huge list of them on my site so you and the adults in your life can learn more about nature.

Head to www.RaisingLifelongLearners.com/NatureScienceResources to find cool links to things like:

- Live animal cams that rock
- Virtual field trips you'll love
- Book lists that will keep you busy for ages
- Amazing documentaries to watch about nature
- Sensational tools for your nature exploration toolkit
- Extension ideas so you can become an expert on anything in this book
- Nature science clubs to join or programs to take part in
- More citizen science projects to be a part of so you can change the world
- Scavenger hunts and craft ideas to challenge your mind
- And so much more . . .

ACKNOWLEDGMENTS

Books are big projects, but so much fun to bring to life. When you do big things, you need big support from family, friends and experts. I've been so blessed to have support like that.

Your family is probably pretty cool, but mine REALLY rocks! My kiddos put up with my late nights, the sleep-in mornings that followed, lots of frozen pizza and daily science experiments (though they enjoyed that part). My husband cheered me on, grocery shopped and held down the fort while I spent endless hours hiding out on my computer. He even pretended to be excited when the butterfly eggs we had on our kitchen table hatched earlier than expected and we had what seemed like hundreds of teeny tiny caterpillars crawling around!

And I have some pretty amazing friends, too. Lori, Cait, Cristy and Dianna are the best cheerleaders a girl could have. My buddies on the 2:1 team were an incredible support system—thanks Aurie, Cheryl, Marci, Amy and Lisa. I love you girls.

Did you get a load of the gorgeous pictures in this book? Melissa Lennig is absolutely amazing and her boys were such fun to work with on these projects.

You know, when you hold a book in your hand, there are a bunch of people whose hard work went into making it spectacular. Sarah Monroe is a fantastic editor with an eye for detail that makes an author shine (thanks for making me shine, Sarah). Page Street Publishing produces stunning books thanks to the vision of publisher Will Kiester and all the great people on their design, editorial and production teams.

I am so grateful for all of the kiddos that came over to explore and discover backyard nature science with me, and agreed to get their hair done by Lori Bryant of hairbylori.com and pictures taken in the cool, fun, bright clothes that the amazing mamas behind Primary.com were gracious enough to give them. I can't get over how fun those clothes were to mix and match, and how easily they all washed up after long afternoons in the dirt playing with frogs and bugs. I had so much fun with you all—Trevor, Molly, Logan, Isaac, Owen, Colin, Hope, Elijah, Mark, Victoria, Benjamin and Jonathan. You are the best backyard nature scientists I could ever ask for!

Finally, I can't begin to thank all of the bloggers, readers and online friends who have supported Raising Lifelong Learners and Raising Poppies over the last few years. You have no idea how much each and every one of you mean to me. Your stories, your kids' stories and your kindness inspire me every single day.

ABOUT THE AUTHOR

Colleen Kessler is an explorer, tinkerer, educator, creator and a passionate advocate for the needs of gifted and twice-exceptional children. She has a B.S. in elementary education, a M.Ed. in gifted studies and is the founder of the popular blog Raising Lifelong Learners.

The author of more than a dozen books for teachers, parents and kids, Colleen left teaching after more than a decade to write and speak about parenting, education, giftedness and hands-on learning and play. You can find out more about upcoming appearances on her website.

Colleen loves hiking, playing in the dirt, reading, dreaming, playing games and creating fun activities and science experiments to do with her four fantastic children. Homeschooling is an adventure she hadn't planned on, but she is embracing the opportunity to learn alongside her kids every day, and inspiring other parents to do the same.

She lives in northeast Ohio where there are plenty of parks and the shores of Lake Erie to explore with her kids and her amazing husband. Or . . . she just might be in her backyard watching the kids play, catching ladybugs or building fairy gardens.

You can always find her online at RaisingLifelongLearners.com and on social media @ColleenKessler. Get in touch with her at RaisingLifelongLearners.com/Contact

INDEX